The Power Of Impartation

Written by Michael C King

This book and other titles by Michael King can be found at TheKingsofEden.com

Available from Amazon.com, Createspace.com, and other retail outlets.

ISBN-13: 978-1-946252-07-4

OTHER TITLES BY MICHAEL C KING:

Gemstones From Heaven - God Signs Series Book 1
Feathers From Heaven - God Signs Series Book 2

Faith to Raise the Dead - Abundant Life Series Book 1

The Gamer's Guide to the Kingdom of God
Practical Keys to Raise the Dead

COLLABORATIONS AND ANTHOLOGIES

Broken To Whole
God Speaks

Table of Contents

Dedication

I dedicate this book to Holy Spirit, who imparts to us all.

"There are different kinds of gifts, but the same Spirit distributes them. . . All these are the work of one and the same Spirit, and he distributes them to each one, just as he determines." 1 Corinthians 12:4, 9

Preface

When I first sat down to write *The Power of Impartation*, it was actually just a blog post, and I aim to keep blog posts under two pages long. By the time I finished writing the initial article, I was already having to split it into a three-part series, and by the time I had published that, my writing on the subject had ballooned even further. It felt like I was being reminded at every turn of more and more relevant information, spiritual encounters, scripture verses, profound insights, and more. I could have continued adding to the series online, but having published an overly-long blog series in the past, I decided this would be better in a book—a book full of teaching and insight on impartation.

The ultimate goal of this book is to help the believer accelerate his or her growth in spiritual power. This means more healings, miracles, stronger faith, and much more. Jesus said in John 14:11 that if we are unable to believe in His words, we should believe the evidence of the miracles themselves. If we are honest with ourselves, the Christian walk is supposed to be one that involves demonstrations of power—signs, wonders, and miracles. Jesus modeled these things along with casting out demons, divine healing, and much more in his earthly ministry. Then, He commissioned us to perform these acts and teach others to do the same. Through a better grasp of the tool of impartation, this book will help the reader do these things and more.

To accomplish this, we are going to get into the details: what impartation is, the mechanisms of how it functions, and how we can make intentional use of these principles to accelerate our own spiritual growth and see prayers answered faster. We are going to identify how we can help others do the same, and how we can even use it in the setting of a larger community so everyone grows at an accelerated rate. We are going to look at ways we can facilitate receiving downloads from heaven and how that helps us engage the impartation process, as well as some of the potential pitfalls or areas of caution on the journey. Finally, I am going to cast some vision on how we can work toward building a spiritual culture where powerful encounters with the Holy Spirit can become more common through the keys that impartation provides us. We have a lot to cover, so I encourage you to turn the page and let the journey begin!

Chapter 1

You Have Something To Give

In order to get the most out of a book called *The Power of Impartation* it is helpful to know what impartation is and how it works, so that's where we are going to start. After all, what is impartation? Where is it in the Bible? And how do we know we can do it? Let's open up the scriptures and take a look.

SPIRITUAL LAWS

Before we can truly begin to discuss impartation, which is in fact a spiritual law on its own, we need to take a look at a few spiritual laws and how they interplay with one another. To explain, spiritual laws are much like natural laws that govern how creation works—things like gravity and entropy. They are a series of rules that impassively govern how physical creation functions. Likewise, spiritual laws are impartial and govern how the spiritual realms function, but due to being higher laws than physical ones, they have a trickle-down effect to the physical world as well. The first is the Law of Sowing and Reaping, which we will cover in more depth later in this book. In short, this law recognizes that whatever we put out, or "sow," we will receive back in like kind—we "reap" it. This is where the saying "you reap what you sow" comes from, meaning that whatever one puts out, that is what they will receive in return. 2 Corinthians 9:6 says, "Remember this: Whoever sows sparingly will also reap sparingly, and whoever sows generously will also reap generously." The extent to which we sow out will dictate what and how we receive in return. Monetary investments work in this manner, in that a small investment should yield a small return whereas a large investment is expected to yield a far greater monetary return—and barring unexpected circumstances, that is precisely how it happens. This doesn't just work with finances, however, as Proverbs 14:14 relates, "The faithless will be fully repaid for their ways, and the good rewarded for theirs." In other words, it isn't just money that is subject to the Law of Sowing and Reaping, but literally everything in all creation, even our thoughts, feelings, words, and deeds.

There is one major sticking point with this law, however, and that is the issue of effort. Because the returns we get are largely dependent on our output, there are limitations in place. In fact, God addresses those limitations and tells us He will go above and beyond them, but even that is conditional. Ephesians 3:20 says, "Now to him who is able to do immeasurably more than all we ask or imagine, according to his power that is at work within us . . ." While this verse promises us that God will do *more* than we can ask or think, the condition stated there is that it is *according to the power at work within us.* In other words, our sowing and reaping has a direct impact on what God does on our behalf. And even though God *does* do far more than we can expect, it doesn't change the fact that *we* are often the limiting factor to what we receive from Him, and this is primarily due to the Law of Sowing and Reaping. Now, while some might make the argument that Jesus already took care of that on the cross and we get everything regardless of what we sow or reap, I suggest an in-depth review of the scriptures do not support this view completely. Did Jesus pay the price to destroy all negative cycles of sowing and reaping? Yes. Does that mean it happens automatically? Sometimes. The rest of the time we have to expend effort on our part to *apply* it to our lives. There is a reason Philippians 2:12 says to ". . . continue to work out your salvation . . ." We don't work to earn salvation, but we do sometimes need to expend effort to successfully apply it and receive its benefits. Keep this in mind as we go through this book, as much of what we are going to discuss is focused on how we can intentionally engage spiritual laws with our effort. None of that negates what Jesus did on the cross but neither does the work of the cross negate the value of what is shared here. In fact, the cross is what makes it all possible. How? Let's discuss another law and find out.

The Law of Sowing and Reaping has its limitations, as stated previously, in that what we receive is based on our efforts and output. There is another law, however, that does not operate on the principle of input and output, and this is what we receive freely in Christ: The Law of Inheritance.

The beautiful thing about the Law of Inheritance is that it has nothing whatsoever to do with our effort. In fact, one might suggest that it is a higher law in that we reap where we have *not* sown because we receive the benefits of what someone *else* has done. We see this in John 4:35-38 where Jesus has just spoken with the Samaritan woman at the well. She leaves and then Jesus instructs his disciples, saying:

> Don't you have a saying, 'It's still four months until harvest'? I tell you, open your eyes and look at the fields! They are ripe for harvest. Even now the one who reaps draws a wage and harvests a crop for eternal life, so that the sower and the reaper may be glad together. Thus the saying 'One sows and another reaps' is true. I sent you to reap what you have not worked for. Others have done the hard work, and you have reaped the benefits of their labor" (John 4:35-38).

Jesus explains quite clearly to them that it is possible for one person to sow and for another to reap, and this is exactly how inheritance works. In human terms, who is it that earns an inheritance for a son or daughter? The parents do. What do the children do to earn that inheritance? Absolutely nothing. They receive it simply because of who they are—due to the nature of their relationship with their parents.

It isn't just tangible things that we can inherit either—even generational blessings and curses are inherited. It's not something we earned, it's something we receive because of who we are in relation to our ancestors. It's due to our bloodline, ancestry, or heritage—all different ways of expressing the same thing. Likewise, we get all the inheritance of Jesus, but not because we did anything to earn it. In fact, it was impossible for us to earn what He paid for with His blood, and if we *had* earned it then it wouldn't, by definition, be an inheritance. It instead would be wages that we worked for and earned. Romans 6:23 tells us, "For the wages of sin is death, but the gift of God is eternal life in Christ Jesus our Lord." Wages are something we earn, but inheritance is a gift, something that is not earned, and we receive an inheritance in Christ that allows us to live sin-free forever in Him. Yet, that is just one *part* of what we receive from Him.

In Christ we have been gifted with a new nature, His nature, and we have been adopted and grafted in as sons and daughters of God. This means that we now get to freely receive the inheritance of God our Father in heaven. So how do we make use of the Law of Inheritance in our lives? It is about walking in authority as sons and daughters of God. When we understand our identity and inheritance, we can freely operate in our kingly authority and properly utilize what has been given to us.

So what does this have to do with a book on the Power of Impartation? The Law of Impartation is actually a subsidiary law underneath the Law of Inheritance, in that it functions based off of giving something away for free. Those who receive it do so freely and it costs them nothing to obtain. We can make use of the Law of Sowing and Reaping to enhance its effects, which we will review later, but for now let's take a deeper look at impartation and how it works.

IMPARTATION

Impartation by definition is the giving of something from one person to another. Generally it is used in a more ethereal manner—giving of knowledge or spiritual power, not pertaining to tangible things. If I were to give someone an apple, we do not typically say that I "imparted" an apple to that person; however, if I were to teach them something, we might say that I "imparted" knowledge to them. The point here is that impartation carries with it a connotation of giving something, but generally something incorporeal. Intangible is not synonymous with worthless as we can give non-physical things to one another that are often highly valuable. Colleges and universities, responsible for imparting knowledge, are rather expensive—largely because people value the information that comes from them. When someone wants to learn something, they are often willing to pay money to learn that information or skill—all of which indicate how intangible things can have immense value.

Likewise, spiritual things can also have great value. In 1 Timothy 4:8a Paul said to Timothy, "For physical training is of some value, but Godliness has value for all things. . . ." The apostle Paul valued impartation somewhat highly if his opening in the letter to the church in Rome is any indication. He mentioned it in Romans 1:11, saying "I long to see you so that I may impart to you some spiritual gift to make you strong. . . ." The word "impart" used here is the Greek word *metadidōmi* which means "to share or give" (Strong). The reason I point that out is we need to understand that when we impart something spiritual, we are literally giving something to someone. We are passing on some amount of spiritual gift, grace, virtue, or empowerment from person to person. In this passage we see that Paul wanted to share a spiritual gift with the church in Rome. Paul wasn't wondering *if* he could do it, but already recognized that he could, and he valued it enough that it was part of why he wanted to make a trip to see the Roman church.

Ultimately, impartation is the means by which we can pass on spiritual qualities from one person to another, and we can see it displayed throughout scripture multiple times more than the above passage. We are going to look at a few of those places now and how they relate to sharing of spiritual grace from one to another—both so we have a context of where it is in the Bible and to lay a foundation for the existence of impartation. We will also review these scriptures again later on in this book to pull out some other key information they hold.

One of the most notable places we see impartation in scripture is in Numbers 11, where Moses is overwhelmed by the duties of running a nation. God had a solution for the problem. It says:

> The Lord said to Moses: "Bring me seventy of Israel's elders who are known to you as leaders and officials among the people. Have them come to the tent of meeting, that they may stand there with you. I will come down and speak with you there, and I will take some of the power of the Spirit that is on you and put it on them. They will share the burden of the people with you so that you will not have to carry it alone." . . . . So Moses went out and told the people what the Lord had said. He brought together seventy of their elders

and had them stand around the tent. Then the Lord came down in the cloud and spoke with him, and he took some of the power of the Spirit that was on him and put it on the seventy elders. When the Spirit rested on them, they prophesied—but did not do so again. However, two men, whose names were Eldad and Medad, had remained in the camp. They were listed among the elders, but did not go out to the tent. Yet the Spirit also rested on them, and they prophesied in the camp." (Numbers 11:16-17, 24-26)

One of the interesting things in that passage is that God was the one who came up with the suggestion to impart what was on Moses and share it with the others—which suggests that not only is God okay with it, but that He recognized there was a spiritual substance of some kind on Moses's life that both needed to be moved and *could* be moved! If we think about it, that's kind of groundbreaking all on its own. Hebrews 11:1 tells us that faith is a substance, so why couldn't other spiritual things be substances as well? We see this concept where impartation revolves around a substance, what I call "spirit matter," in other scriptures as well. In 2 Kings 2:9-10 it says:

> When they had crossed, Elijah said to Elisha, "Tell me, what can I do for you before I am taken from you?"
>
> "Let me inherit a double portion of your spirit," Elisha replied.
>
> "You have asked a difficult thing," Elijah said, "yet if you see me when I am taken from you, it will be yours— otherwise, it will not."

The way Elijah and Elisha talked about passing on "portions" of Elijah's spirit, it seems like they knew something about how spiritual forces function that we have long since forgotten. Elijah didn't shoot down his disciple's request—he gave conditions under which it would occur. The prophet knew that something of the essence of his spirit *could* be passed on—and if we read further in that passage, we see that the conditions were met and indeed portions of his spirit *were* passed on.

If we want to be able to understand how impartation works, why it works, or even how it can be useful, we need to truly grasp that we are discussing spirit matter. People often refer to faith as some kind of airy idea or this intangible quality of the mind, but when we are dealing with passing virtue on from one person to another, the idea that faith is a substance is of key importance. Why? If faith is just an idea then it has value but that value is limited—you can't give something tangible to someone if you don't have it. If, however, it is indeed a spiritual substance that we can do something with, then its potential applications widen significantly. I talk about faith as a substance here not because it is the only kind of spirit matter, but because the scriptures clearly state that it has substance where it does not say the same about other spiritual things. Thus, it serves as an important example for the existence of spirit matter.

Many years ago, I was at a spiritual training school in Harrisburg, PA and was living in an apartment in the back half of a 24/7 prayer house. One evening my roommates were elsewhere and I had the place to myself so I turned the lights off and was spending some time chatting with God in the dark. God started telling me about object permanence in the spirit and demonstrated by having an angel walk in the room holding a candle. I was seeing this angel in the spirit, not physically, but he walked across the room, set the candle on the coffee table, and walked off. What the Lord showed me was that if nobody removed that candle from the table, it would be there forever—and even if I never saw the candle in the spirit again, it wouldn't stop being there. For all I know, over a decade later, that candle is still there. Another way of thinking about this is by looking at angels and swords. Often, people who see angels see them carrying a sword. Is the sword an angel carries a real object or is it just pretend? I suggest it is real, but not made of physical matter. This spiritual sword is used by an angel to fight other spirit beings and to attack and defend against their weapons—it is far more than a concept. The shield of faith spoken of in Ephesians 6:16 is not a physical object, nor are the flaming darts it defends against—but they are still objects nonetheless. They don't stop being spiritual matter just because we can't physically touch them. In the same way, the things we give or receive in the spirit are actual things, which also means one must actually *have* them to give in the first place. We will discuss how we can give away things we do not yet possess later in the book, but let's take a look at a key example of what I am referring to.

One day Peter and John were going up to the temple at the time of prayer—at three in the afternoon. Now a man who was lame from birth was being carried to the temple gate called Beautiful, where he was put every day to beg from those going into the temple courts. When he saw Peter and John about to enter, he asked them for money. Peter looked straight at him, as did John. Then Peter said, "Look at us!" So the man gave them his attention, expecting to get something from them.

Then Peter said, "Silver or gold I do not have, but what I do have I give you. In the name of Jesus Christ of Nazareth, walk." Taking him by the right hand, he helped him up, and instantly the man's feet and ankles became strong. He jumped to his feet and began to walk. Then he went with them into the temple courts, walking and jumping, and praising God. (Acts 3:1-8)

Peter's word choice there has always been fascinating to me. "Silver or gold I do not have, but *what I do have* I give you." Peter recognized the beggar wanted material goods, and also knew that he did not possess what the man was asking for. Yet, Peter knew he had something he *could* give the man—and as the passage reveals, Peter did just that. Think about how profound that is. Peter knew that he possessed within his being a substance that he could pass to the other man, and this was something powerful—so powerful it had the ability to heal the lame man's legs so he could walk!

While there are a few different scriptures where virtue is clearly passed from one person to another,[1] the above passage brings us to another important question—what kinds of things can we give away and receive? We have seen above that healing can be passed on in this manner, and Moses showed us that the spiritual capacity to govern a nation can also be transferred. Elijah and Elisha showed us we can pass on some measure of the virtue resident within our spirits one to another. The Bible also reveals we can give the gifts of the Holy Spirit to one another. Romans 1:11 says, "I long to see you so that I may impart to you some spiritual gift to make you strong. . . ." Paul the apostle wanted to visit the Church of Rome so he could impart spiritual gifts to them, so clearly those are things we can pass on as well. In John 20:22 Jesus breathed on his disciples, releasing the Holy Spirit upon them.

There are some other interesting passages involving imparting things one to another, but I want us to take a look back in Genesis 27 and see the exchange between Isaac and his two sons, Esau and Jacob. In this passage we see Isaac being deceived by his wife

---

[1] Mark 5:30, Luke 8:46 are two others

Rebekah and his son Jacob to swindle Esau's blessing so Jacob would get it—but the conversation between Isaac and Esau shortly thereafter has some fascinating implications:

> . . . Jacob brought it [the food] to him and he ate; and he brought some wine and he drank. Then his father Isaac said to him, "Come here, my son, and kiss me." So he went to him and kissed him. When Isaac caught the smell of his clothes, he blessed him and said,
>
> "Ah, the smell of my son is like the smell of a field that the Lord has blessed. May God give you heaven's dew and earth's richness—an abundance of grain and new wine. May nations serve you and peoples bow down to you. Be lord over your brothers, and may the sons of your mother bow down to you. May those who curse you be cursed and those who bless you be blessed."
>
> After Isaac finished blessing him, and Jacob had scarcely left his father's presence, his brother Esau came in from hunting. He too prepared some tasty food and brought it to his father. Then he said to him, "My father, please sit up and eat some of my game, so that you may give me your blessing."
>
> His father Isaac asked him, "Who are you?"
>
> "I am your son," he answered, "your firstborn, Esau."
>
> Isaac trembled violently and said, "Who was it, then, that hunted game and brought it to me? I ate it just before you came and I blessed him—and indeed he will be blessed!"
>
> When Esau heard his father's words, he burst out with a loud and bitter cry and said to his father, "Bless me—me too, my father!"
>
> But he said, "Your brother came deceitfully and took your blessing."

Esau said, "Isn't he rightly named Jacob? This is the second time he has taken advantage of me: He took my birthright, and now he's taken my blessing!" Then he asked, "Haven't you reserved any blessing for me?"

Isaac answered Esau, "I have made him lord over you and have made all his relatives his servants, and I have sustained him with grain and new wine. So what can I possibly do for you, my son?"

Esau said to his father, "Do you have only one blessing, my father? Bless me too, my father!" Then Esau wept aloud. (Genesis 27:25-38)

This passage is a bit lengthy, so we will summarize key points and look at significant things they said. First, Jacob pretends to be Esau so Isaac (who was blind) will bless him instead of his brother, and when Esau shows up later, Isaac tells him that he *already gave the blessing away*. This means that first, Isaac *had* something nontangible to give away. Second, he, Rebekah, Jacob, and Esau all knew it. Third, when Esau showed up, Isaac's response was essentially, "I gave it all away already and don't have anything left to give you" because he didn't have it any longer—Esau's brother did. Esau literally wept about this. That's not something you do if the incorporeal thing you were going to receive doesn't exist, doesn't matter, or if there are multiples of it. Esau was very clear that his father only had one real blessing to give (which in that culture always went to the firstborn son), and that he was swindled out of it. We will look at the subject of blessing as a form of impartation in a later chapter, but it is of note here that at least in the Old Testament, there was a limited quantity of blessing to give. If Isaac had enough blessing to give both sons, he presumably would have. In fact, we see a similar situation in Genesis 48 with Joseph's sons Ephraim and Manasseh receiving a blessing from Israel (formerly known as Jacob). Under the New Testament, however, we don't have the same limitation issue—but we will cover why that is in a future chapter as well.

Ultimately, it seems almost any spiritual substance can be passed on one to another through the process of impartation, and while that might not sound very useful to some, let us not forget that Peter made use of this capacity while healing a man. If it has the ability to release the healing power of God from one person to another, I think we need to give it a closer look. In the following chapter we are going to look at how the human spirit is a vessel for God's power, how the Holy Spirit co-labors with our spirits to grow God's power within us, and how that relates to impartation.

Chapter 2

Impartation and the Human Spirit

Our interaction with God is largely a partnership between us and the Holy Spirit, and it is precisely that interaction we are going to explore. We are going to consider the influence and interaction between the human spirit, the Holy Spirit, and how they are related to impartation—as well as how we can benefit from understanding it better. For this to make sense, we need to begin by reviewing a bit about the human spirit.

The Bible tells us in Romans 8:11 that the Holy Spirit has been given to each follower of Jesus, but if we read just a little further in that passage it says something fascinating. Romans 8:16 states, "The Spirit Himself testifies with our spirit that we are children of God." Why is that fascinating? The evidence of partnership. It isn't just the Holy Spirit speaking of something, or our spirits testifying of the same, but *both together.* This means that not only are our human spirits involved in the process, but it is an active partnership between us and the Holy Spirit. We need to understand this connection to gain the best understanding of how impartation works.

The human spirit is something that we have been innately given upon creation by God. In fact, we could even make the case that when humankind (beginning in Adam) first received spirits, we received them through the process of impartation. Genesis 2:7 says,

"Then the Lord God formed man of dust from the ground, and breathed into his nostrils the breath of life; and man became a living being." If we consider that impartation is the process of taking spiritual substance and passing it from one to another, God did exactly that when He took of His own Spirit and released it into the body of the man He had just created. The result? Life. When we consider mankind's spiritual origins, the divine essence and nature of God being intentionally injected into a human body, it makes sense that as God's children we would possess similar abilities, including the ability to pass spiritual substances from one of us to another.

We need to recognize that our spirits are actually an integral part of our existence, are different than the soul (which is the realm of the mind, will, and emotions), and that our spirits experience this reality both separately and in conjunction with our souls and bodies. It is strange to word it that way, but in the same way God is Holy Spirit, Father, and Son, we also have a spirit, soul, and body, and they work in conjunction with one another. We see this classification of the different aspects of our humanity echoed in scripture as well. Isaiah 38:16 says, "Lord, by such things people live; and my spirit finds life in them too. You restored me to health and let me live." Isaiah is talking about how his body is restored to health, but also that his spirit finds life as well, acknowledging the unique experience that his spirit has as compared to his body. I have a few reasons for emphasizing the presence and existence of the human spirit, and they all relate in some way to impartation and the Holy Spirit.

In 2 Corinthians 4:7 it says, "But we have this treasure in earthen vessels, so that the surpassing greatness of the power will be of God and not from ourselves . . ." The spiritual power that exists within us ultimately comes from God, and for us to get the most out of this subject we need to understand that our human spirit functions as a vessel for God's power. We will look at how that works in the next chapter, but for now, remember that God's power resides in us and our spirit is the carrying container for that power. When the Holy Spirit wants to do something with us, it is in connection with our spirit. In fact, we see this connection expressed quite clearly in Paul's first letter to the Corinthian church. There is an important principle in 1 Corinthians 14 that displays the link between the Holy Spirit and our human spirit. The passage is talking about tongues and prophecy, but pay attention to what it says about the human spirit:

> For if I pray in a tongue, my spirit prays, but my mind is unfruitful. So what shall I do? I will pray with my spirit, but I will also pray with my understanding; I will sing with my spirit, but I will also sing with my understanding. Otherwise when you are praising God in the Spirit, how can someone else, who is now put in the position of an inquirer, say "Amen" to your thanksgiving, since they do not know what you are saying? You are giving thanks well enough, but no one else is edified. . . . Two or three prophets should speak, and the others should weigh carefully what is said. And if a revelation comes to someone who is sitting down, the first speaker should stop. For you can all prophesy in turn so that everyone may be instructed and encouraged. The spirits of prophets are subject to the control of prophets. (2 Corinthians 14:14-17, 29-32)

As I previously mentioned, this passage is talking about prophecy and tongues, both gifts of the Holy Spirit, but I want to emphasize that Paul is talking in this passage about people praying with *their own spirits*. He explains in 1 Corinthians 14:2, "For anyone who speaks in a tongue does not speak to people but to God. Indeed, no one understands them; they utter mysteries by the Spirit." In other words, when we pray in tongues, it is both our spirit and the Holy Spirit working together and it is the interchange between the two that causes something to happen—not just the work of one or the other. Also of note is that Paul clearly states the spirits of the prophets are subject to their own control, which means our human spirits are not simply passively receiving whatever God is doing but we have the ability to control our spirits' actions.

I want us to come back shortly and look at why the interchange between our spirit and the Holy Spirit is important, but to best understand it we need to take another look at Numbers 11:16-17, 24-26 where God helped Moses impart some of his ruling authority and ability onto Israel's elders. To review, it says:

> The Lord said to Moses: "Bring me seventy of Israel's elders who are known to you as leaders and officials among the people. Have them come to the tent of meeting, that they may stand there with you. I will come down and speak with you there, and I will take some of the power of the Spirit that is on you and put it on them. They will share the burden of the people with you so that you will not have to carry it alone." . . . So Moses went out and told the people what the Lord had said. He brought together seventy of their elders and had them stand around the tent. Then the Lord came down in the cloud and spoke with him, and he took some of the power of the Spirit that was on him and put it on the seventy elders. When the Spirit rested on them, they prophesied—but did not do so again. However, two men, whose names were Eldad and Medad, had remained in the camp. They were listed among the elders, but did not go out to the tent. Yet the Spirit also rested on them, and they prophesied in the camp." (Numbers 11:16-17, 24-26)

In addition to the fact that God was the one who instructed Moses in the impartation process, this suggests that not only is God okay with impartation as I mentioned elsewhere, but that He recognized there was a spiritual substance of some kind on Moses's life that needed to be moved. Even more fascinating to me is that God recognized that something He had placed upon Moses had a few different qualities:

1) It helped Moses accomplish something (which in this instance was governing)
2) It could be shared and/or given to others
3) It is possible to share it with someone who is not physically present
4) The "it" being shared is actually part of the nature of God, not just an object
5) Moses was a vessel for the qualities God wanted to pass on, and God had to take some of it *from* Moses in order to share it instead of just providing more of it from heaven.

It is of note that because the process of impartation is sharing an aspect or quality of the Holy Spirit, it means that the qualities of God can be split up. What I mean by that is that while having the Holy Spirit indwelling us means we have *theoretical* access to all aspects of His being at any time, it doesn't mean that all of those aspects are *actively* resident or at work within us. Furthermore, something about impartation causes those qualities to be shared, revealed, or otherwise manifested when they previously were not. The main difference between the Old and New Testament regarding this is that the Holy Spirit is now resident without limit in all believers when previously that was not the case, yet the similarity is that all of His qualities are still not made immediately manifest upon salvation—hence the value and benefit of impartation from one person to another. Why is this important, and how does it relate to the connection between our spirits and the Holy Spirit? Because the Holy Spirit indwells us, we don't have the same limitations placed upon us that Old Testament figures did. We will explore that idea further in a coming chapter, but understand for now that the premise we are working with is that we can give limitlessly without loss on our end.

There is more to explore on the subject of the human spirit and how it connects with impartation again in another Old Testament passage, between Elijah and Elisha. While we covered this passage in the previous chapter as well, there is something unique about these verses which reveal that our human spirit is involved in the impartation process. In 2 Kings 2:9-10 it says:

> "When they had crossed, Elijah said to Elisha, 'Tell me, what can I do for you before I am taken from you?'
>
> 'Let me inherit a double portion of your spirit,' Elisha replied.
>
> 'You have asked a difficult thing,' Elijah said, 'yet if you see me when I am taken from you, it will be yours—otherwise, it will not.'"

Note here that Elisha didn't ask for a double portion of the Holy Spirit that was upon Elijah, but a double portion of *Elijah's* spirit. Furthermore, Elijah didn't say that was impossible, but outlined conditions under which Elisha's request would be granted because what he asked *was* possible. Elisha seemed aware that what he was going to receive had a connection not just to the Spirit of God, but to Elijah's spirit. We see this re-emphasized a few verses later in 2 Kings 2:15 where it says, "The company of the prophets from

Jericho, who were watching, said, 'The spirit of Elijah is resting on Elisha.' And they went to meet him and bowed to the ground before him." Think about that. What would it mean if Elijah's spirit was *literally* resting on his successor? That isn't a figurative statement any more than every time the Bible says that the Holy Spirit literally descended on or rested upon someone. Elijah explained to Elisha how he could obtain two portions of Elijah's spirit, and a group of other prophets later confirmed that it indeed took place.

An angel appeared to Zechariah in Luke 1 and referenced this concept as well, saying in Luke 1:17a, "he will go on before the LORD, in the spirit and power of Elijah. . . ." If angelic messengers from Heaven recognize that it is possible to inherit something from another *person's* spirit and not just from the Holy Spirit, especially when the angels' primary message is clearly confirmed as true and accurate in scripture, we would do well to listen to and learn from the things they have shared.

If we want to understand how impartation works, we have to grasp the concept that our human spirit is involved in a partnership with the Holy Spirit. As a result, one of the things that can happen when we impart to one another is that some aspect of the "flavor" of our spirit can get passed on—because as mentioned earlier, our spirit is the vessel. God's power isn't just dwelling within us, but when it comes in contact with our spirit it has the potential to become part of us. When that occurs, if we are passing that virtue on to others, a small measure of the creativity and divinity of God and other things found in our own lives tends to get mixed in. On occasion this can be a bad thing, and we will discuss that in Chapter 10, but in most cases it is a positive, whereby we get to receive from the grace of God on someone else's life that helps him or her to live for God. While impartation is generally the power of the Holy Spirit passed on, in some ways we are giving the gift of ourselves as well—

and yet, because the Holy Spirit flows like a river through us, we don't have to experience loss on our end even as we give freely of Him and of ourselves to others.

I first discovered that we have the ability to pass on aspects of our own spirit during the impartation process back in the late fall of 2006. I was volunteering at Global Awakening's yearly Voice of the Apostles conference as a result of being in the ministry school of the church where the conference was being held. After one of the night sessions I was tasked with driving one of the speakers, Larry Randolph, and his wife back to their hotel. We had some brief conversation on the ride there, and during that time I asked him if he would mind praying for me to receive an impartation of the prophetic. He agreed, but then we stopped off at a nearby gas station and sub shop, got sidetracked, and the prayer didn't occur that night. I was disappointed, but given that most speakers often have a lot of people vying for their time and energy, I wanted to be respectful of that and didn't push the matter. What happened the next day taught me something interesting about how the flavor of the human spirit is included in the impartation process.

Larry was the speaker for the afternoon session that next day, and after accurately calling out words of knowledge and prophesying over certain audience members which the Holy Spirit highlighted to him, he was about to end, saying "I've got time for one more." Larry then looked directly at me and called me up to the front to pray an impartation of the prophetic over me. Given that his eyesight was bad at the time (which he had announced from the podium), he didn't recognize me, and at first he even said he wasn't sure why he felt led to pray for me. When I reminded him that I had asked him for prayer for that very thing the night prior, he recognized me, chuckled, laid a hand on me and prayed for me to receive an infilling of all of the prophetic gifts and abilities that were resident in his life, and then he closed the session.

I was touched that God heard and honored my request from the previous night, but what followed immediately after that prayer fascinated me. Right after Larry Randolph prayed for me, I had the distinct impression that I needed to take some time in prayer with God, but I was still pretty new to the prophetic as a whole. Had I been a little more seasoned I would have listened better and done just that, but a friend came up immediately and asked me to pray for her as well, which I did. What she actually said was "Hey, you gotta share!" which I did, praying that she would also receive that which Larry passed on to me. The thing was, when I began praying for her and then started prophesying over her, I found that I was speaking very similarly to how Larry prophesied over people. I was using similar phrasing and even how I inflected parts of my sentences was alike. It wasn't that I was being controlled from afar by Larry somehow, but that when he prayed for me to receive the grace of God that was upon his life, it was like I got Larry-Randolph-flavored prophetic unction. This didn't just happen with one person either. I prayed for three or four others and the exact same thing happened. In hindsight, I should have listened to the nudging I felt, as I believe that instead of gaining all of it, I passed some on to others without retaining as much of what was given to me. That experience showed me that there really is something about our own spirit that is involved in the impartation process, and the scriptures confirm it is indeed true. While that may seem strange to some, isn't pouring out our lives for others part of the example Jesus gave us? With impartation, we just give of ourselves in a different manner.

Chapter 3

The Mechanism of Impartation

In the previous chapter we discussed how both the Holy Spirit and our human spirits are involved in the impartation process. As I explained initially, impartation is the means by which we can pass spiritual virtue from one to another. This is possible in part due to the capacity of the human spirit as a vessel for divine power, but also because of the spiritual rules in creation that make this exchange possible. To get the most out of this ability, it seems best to understand how passing spiritual virtue from one person to another works, what happens with what we are given, and how we can maximize its use.

We briefly touched on the idea that in the Old Testament when they would impart something, it seemed the giver no longer possessed it. As New Testament believers we are not under that same limitation! Before we look at how we impart from one to another and how we can use what we receive, I want to explore how the Holy Spirit allows us to give to one another endlessly. The river found in Ezekiel 47:1-5 is a good illustration of how the Holy Spirit works within and through us in this manner. It says:

> The man brought me back to the entrance to the temple, and I saw water coming out from under the threshold of the

temple toward the east (for the temple faced east). The water was coming down from under the south side of the temple, south of the altar. He then brought me out through the north gate and led me around the outside to the outer gate facing east, and the water was trickling from the south side.

As the man went eastward with a measuring line in his hand, he measured off a thousand cubits and then led me through water that was ankle-deep. He measured off another thousand cubits and led me through water that was knee-deep. He measured off another thousand and led me through water that was up to the waist. He measured off another thousand, but now it was a river that I could not cross, because the water had risen and was deep enough to swim in—a river that no one could cross.

If we consider this spiritual encounter as an analogy for us individually, where we are the temple of the Holy Spirit, we have water flowing from within us—the same rivers of living water that Jesus mentioned in John 7:38. If we look at the above passage, the water only keeps getting deeper the longer it flows. What this means for us in regards to impartation is that unlike with physical matter, where we give something away and then don't have it anymore, spiritual dynamics work differently. With the Holy Spirit, when we give something away, we get it replenished and can continue to give even more away, never actually suffering any loss on our part.

Another verse that supports the idea we don't lose what we have received and that it just gets replenished is Romans 11:29 which says, ". . .for God's gifts and his call are irrevocable." Another way of translating that verse is that God's gifts and callings are "without repentance." Part of what this verse is telling us is that it doesn't actually matter if we are following God closely or not—the gifts and abilities we have received do not leave us if we fall away from Him, and we actually can't get rid of them once we have them—they are irrevocable, inextricably tied to our spirit. Even when it seems like something is no longer functioning in our lives, it is not that we no longer possess a spiritual gift, but rather that the flow of power behind it that makes it work isn't there. The ability always remains but the power source is not guaranteed—yet, as Jesus told the disciples in John 15, as we remain in the True Vine, Christ and as He remains in us, we will bear much fruit. How this applies to impartation is that *because* the gifts are tied to our spirit, when we impart something to someone what essentially happens is that the Holy Spirit empowers that gift and allows us to duplicate or multiply it, but the initial gift remains with us

I do want to clarify one thing here. While I have mentioned that impartation can be given limitlessly without loss on our part, there is an exception, and that is when we have received something from someone else and have not yet fully assimilated it into our own spirits. To use the example of Larry Randolph praying for me as mentioned in the last chapter, the reason I believe I was led by the Holy Spirit to not pray for others was in order to fully absorb the impartation I had received. Because I did not do that, I believe that I ended up passing some of it on to others while only retaining part of it for myself, whereas if I had been patient and prayed for others later on, I would have been able to pass on more spiritual virtue freely without losing anything on my end. For example, Larry Randolph could impart a hundred times to me or anyone else without losing anything because it is already resident in his life, but if I do not properly assimilate what he gave me before giving it to someone else, there is the chance that I will not retain all of what I received in prayer, passing on to those I pray for. It is essentially the difference between something that is resting upon me temporarily versus something that begins to reside within me. In John 4:14 Jesus tells the Samaritan woman at the well that ". . . whoever drinks the water I give them will never thirst. Indeed, the water I give them will become in them a spring of water welling up to eternal life." This verse demonstrates a principle. Jesus explained that when something gets deep inside us (something that we "drink" into our spirits), it becomes a spring that produces more of itself. The converse of that is that something that rests upon us but is not absorbed into our spirit yet can be depleted. Once it has been absorbed into our spirit, that is when it becomes a river within us.

I am specifically applying this principle to when we have just recently received something through impartation prayer from someone else. Yet, even that requires being led by the Holy Spirit because there is no hard rule stating that we require a certain amount of time to absorb or retain or "drink deep" of what we have received in prayer. We don't yet understand enough of spiritual things to know when no time is needed, an hour is required, or an even longer time set apart from others to fully retain what we have been given from others, but it is the Holy Spirit's job to lead and guide us in those instances as appropriate.

Impartation is often done through the laying on of hands and praying, but it isn't the only way. Sometimes we will receive something by declaration, where someone says something and we receive it. It is even possible to receive impartation from prayers on old video or audio recordings, something I have had happen on multiple occasions. Ultimately, when faith-to-receive is applied to a situation, we have the potential to obtain a gift. Regardless of how it occurs, the mechanism is a transfer of virtue from one person's spirit to another, but what we are receiving is a transfer of the Holy Spirit's power, usually from that person's life to ours. And again, in the transfer he or she doesn't lose anything.

If we recall in Genesis 27 where Esau asked for a second blessing from his father Isaac, Isaac refused because he had already given his one blessing completely away. It is of note here that at least in the Old Testament, there was a limited quantity of blessing to impart. If Isaac had enough blessing to give both sons, we can assume he would have, like most good fathers. Under the New Testament, however, we don't have the same problem because the Holy Spirit is a limitless supply within us, forever replenishing that which we give away. If Isaac had been in the New Testament, he could reasonably have given both of his children that same blessing, and still had blessing left over.

UNDERSTANDING THE MECHANISM

Now that we understand the Holy Spirit is given to us fully and endlessly, why is it that we still seem to have limitation and lack when it comes to our prayers? And how is it that when we impart something to someone, he or she does not usually operate in it to the same level that we have? My theory of the mechanism of impartation will help explain these things.

The Bible likes to refer to spiritual virtue, anointing, gifts, etc. somewhat generally as "oil" throughout scripture, and 2 Corinthians 4:7 tells us that we are like earthenware jars that receive that oil—so let's use that analogy. If our spirit is a vessel and we are filled with the Holy Spirit, then we are a full jar of oil. So what happens when someone prays and imparts something to us considering our jar is already full? Either something happens to cause the jar to expand and catch the new oil being poured in, or nothing happens and the oil overflows, runs down the side, and gets wasted. Expanding clay pots don't exist in the natural, but we're going to stick with the analogy as we are dealing with spiritual realities and our spirits have the ability to expand. When we receive impartation, our spirits expand in some way to catch that which is being imparted upon us, but at that point, one of a few things will happen:

1) We will immediately use up what was imparted at that time (similar to my Larry Randolph story), our vessel will shrink back to normal size, and we will notice no long-term change.
2) We will squander what we have been given and our vessel will go back to normal size with no long-term change.
3) We will tend the oil wisely, assimilate it, and our jar will expand permanently to a new size.

Either we receive the gift of impartation and it becomes permanent, or we receive it but don't absorb it and it may go away. What I have found is that we can influence how permanent it does or does not become. For example, why would I have felt nudged not to pray for someone else after receiving impartation prayer from Larry Randolph? It wouldn't matter unless my actions were able to influence what happened in some meaningful way. The truth is that if we want to get the most out of what we have received freely through prayer, we will need to steward it, assimilate it, and make it our own. Keep in mind again that I am talking about the process of stewarding what we receive from someone else, not whether the giver is limited in their giving.

I am reminded of the parable Jesus told of the five wise and five foolish virgins in Matthew 25. They were all attending a wedding, but the wise virgins brought extra oil for their lamps and the foolish ones didn't bring any. When the foolish virgins needed it, because they had not stewarded theirs wisely, when it was time to be doing something else (being at a wedding), they were having to play catch-up, running out to a merchant to go find some oil. One of the things that I think is poorly understood about the subject of impartation is the issue of stewardship. Impartation is a freely given gift, and it costs us nothing to receive it. However, if we want to get any long-term benefit out of it then we will need to do something in response to what we have been given to tend that which we have received. Many years ago I heard Pastor Bill Johnson of Bethel Church preach a sermon and in it he said something to the effect of "While we get the gifts for free, we will have to pay a price to develop them." Impartation is free. We literally get something for nothing. Yet, if we want to benefit from it long-term, we will have to steward what we have been given.

This is what I am referring to when I say we have to assimilate the impartation we have received. There is something about being purposeful with this process that can make all the difference from a results-perspective. Why are there so many Charismatic conferences and yet so few people walking powerfully in signs, wonders, and miracles? After all, many people have been prayed over and imparted to by scores of big-named preachers who walk actively and powerfully in the anointing of the Holy Spirit, so why isn't everyone walking daily in the miraculous? I think there are a few reasons for this, but the ones primarily relevant to this conversation are the issues of assimilation and stewardship. If we do nothing to retain and develop that which we have been given for free, we should not be surprised when we get nothing out of it in the long-term. If, however, we tend to what we have been given, we will be able to see an increase over time in the flow of the Holy Spirit's power in our lives.

How do we assimilate, absorb, or "tend to" what we have received? I have found that if I spend time in prayer, worship, soaking, or otherwise engaging with God in the subsequent days after receiving impartation prayer, it seems to have a positive impact on whether I retain the impartation or not. In other words, spending time with God and in His presence causes that impartation to adhere itself to our spirit. When we engage the Holy Spirit intentionally, we will observe these benefits more readily—and that should come as no surprise. When we receive prayer like this, we are literally receiving some aspect of the Holy Spirit's nature and power, so going back to the Divine Source to let what we have received fully implant itself strikes me as both natural and wise.

IN SEED FORM

Another analogy we could use to describe the process of impartation is that of planting and watering seeds in a garden. Impartation is generally a process by which we receive a spiritual gift or virtue in seed form. While planting a tree seed will eventually grow a tree, it is not the same thing as transplanting a fully grown tree into a garden. Impartation is usually more like seed-planting, which requires us to tend the seeds in the garden of our spirit so they will grow and yield benefits. Three separate passages come to mind that speak to this issue of tending to and training or growing what we have received freely. The first is Paul's admonition to Timothy in 2 Timothy 1:16 which says, "For this reason I remind you to fan into flame the gift of God, which is in you through the laying on of my hands." Paul told Timothy to fan his gift into flame for a reason. The apostle understood that what he had imparted to Timothy was like a spark or a seed—something that required tending so it could grow into something far greater. The corollary of that is if that seed is not tended to, it is unlikely to grow.

The second passage I am reminded of is the parable of the mustard seed in Matthew 13:31-32 which says:

> . . . The kingdom of heaven is like a mustard seed, which a
> man took and planted in his field. Though it is the smallest

of all seeds, yet when it grows, it is the largest of garden plants and becomes a tree, so that the birds come and perch in its branches.

The issue isn't how much faith or any other empowerment one starts out with. What is important is what it will grow to become when given time and attention. In 1 Timothy 4:7-8 Paul said to Timothy:

Have nothing to do with godless myths and old wives' tales; rather, train yourself to be godly. For physical training is of some value, but godliness has value for all things, holding promise for both the present life and the life to come.

The apostle also wrote in 1 Timothy 4:14, saying "Do not neglect your gift, which was given you through prophecy when the body of elders laid their hands on you." We see here that Paul told Timothy to train to be godly, to fan into flame the gifts he received, and to not neglect his gifts. Why would he tell Timothy these things if there was no purpose, no meaning, and no benefit? Stewardship of the things we receive freely by impartation is highly important if we intend to obtain any value from them.

The third passage I am reminded of is another parable Jesus told—the parable of the sower. Matthew 13:1-9 says:

That same day Jesus went out of the house and sat by the lake. Such large crowds gathered around him that he got into a boat and sat in it, while all the people stood on the shore. Then he told them many things in parables, saying: "A farmer went out to sow his seed. As he was scattering the seed, some fell along the path, and the birds came and ate it up. Some fell on rocky places, where it did not have much soil. It sprang up quickly, because the soil was shallow. But when the sun came up, the plants were scorched, and they withered because they had no root. Other seed fell among thorns, which grew up and choked the plants. Still other seed fell on good soil, where it produced a crop—a hundred, sixty or thirty times what was sown. Whoever has ears, let them hear."

Jesus explains later in that chapter that the seed he was referring to is the gospel message, but the same principles apply to this subject. When seed lands on good soil it grows and produces fruit, but when it lands on poor soil it doesn't, and in some cases, it never takes root to begin with. From a gardening perspective, while some soil is better than others, any soil can be fixed into good ground if tended over time. Sure, bad soil may require more effort, but the key is largely how tended the soil is, not its initial state. Great soil that gets no attention will rapidly be covered in weeds because the growing environment is great for anything, good or bad. If we want to get the most out of impartation, we need to understand that we are a vessel receiving an enlargement, or soil where a seed is planted. If we tend what we have received, we will find ourselves with a vessel that is expanding and with a garden of plants that are heading toward maturity and fruit-bearing status. So long as we tend those things wisely over time, we will see the benefits. Yet if we ignore every seed that is sown it may never get planted, or it may get planted and remain stunted in its growth, unable to flourish. A mighty tree planted in a small pot will never reach its potential—it must have the right environment to grow.

THE "WHO" OF IMPARTATION

One thing that I want to clear up before we go further in the book is the question of who can impart and how we can know if it happens or not. Some people believe that impartation only works if God initiates it. I have not found that to be true. It may be *more effective* in certain instances if God initiates it, but that doesn't mean it doesn't work the rest of the time. In Acts 3:6, Peter said to a cripple that "what I have I give you." He didn't say "what God gave me permission to give you right in this moment." He didn't say "God gives you." Peter clearly said, "What *I have* I give you." Peter recognized that he not only had a spiritual substance but that he could give it to other people at times of *his* choosing.

This idea that we personally get to decide when we impart things or when supernatural acts are performed is a major challenge to the theology of most believers, but it is demonstrated throughout scripture. We see God giving Moses the ability to perform miracles at will in Exodus 4:21. It says, "The Lord said to Moses, 'When you return to Egypt, see that you perform before Pharaoh all the wonders I have given you the power to do.'" God did not place any prohibitions on Moses' use of those abilities, and it literally states that *Moses* had the power to perform them. In Revelation 11 we see the Two Witnesses being given power to do certain miracles whenever they feel like it. Revelation 11:5-6 says:

> If anyone tries to harm them, fire comes from their mouths and devours their enemies. This is how anyone who wants to harm them must die. They have power to shut up the heavens so that it will not rain during the time they are prophesying; and they have power to turn the waters into blood and to strike the earth with every kind of plague as often as they want.

The apostle Paul did this in Acts 19:11-12 as well, where it says, "God performed special miracles through Paul, so that even handkerchiefs and aprons that had touched him were taken to the sick, and their illnesses were cured and the evil spirits left them." The term *"special"* in "special miracles" is made of two Greek words. The first word is *ou* which is a negative term, such as 'no' or 'not'. The second word is *tygchano* which means 'to happen' or 'to chance' (Strong). It basically says "And God performed not-by-chance miracles by the hands of Paul." Another way of thinking of this is "purposeful miracles" or "miracles on purpose" because when something doesn't happen by chance, it is done intentionally.

We even see Jesus doing the same thing. John 6:5-6 says:

> When Jesus looked up and saw a great crowd coming toward him, he said to Philip, "Where shall we buy bread for these people to eat?" He asked this only to test him, for he already had in mind what he was going to do.

Jesus was preaching to the multitudes, knew they needed food, then challenged his disciples with the problem right before performing a multiplication-miracle he was *already planning to perform*. One can only *plan* to perform a miracle if they know they can pull it off. Otherwise they're only *trying* to do one, which is totally different and leaves things up to chance. Jesus planned it because he knew he could perform that miracle whenever he wanted to. In fact, in a separate situation we even see Jesus imparting the Holy Spirit to His disciples in what we could term an "at-will" moment, doing it when He wanted and to whom He wanted. It says in John 20:22 that Jesus breathed on His disciples in order to impart the Holy Spirit to each of them. Now, practically speaking, this means one of a few things.

Either He had them stand in a group, took a deep breath, and blew in their general direction, or what I suspect is more likely given His highly personal ministry style, Jesus did this personally to each one. As He did so, Jesus didn't just breathe on them—he released the *Ruach ha Kodesh* upon them, the *Breath of Life* or *Spirit of Life*, the Holy Spirit of God.

Finally we have Peter and John at the Beautiful Gate in Acts 3. We have already covered this, but Peter intentionally released power to the lame man at a moment of Peter's choosing, as evidenced by the apostle's statement right before the miracle. If Moses, Paul, the Two Witnesses, Jesus, and Peter can all do miracles and perform impartations whenever they want, is there any reason to believe we can't impart gifts one to another at moments of our choosing as well?

We see multiple places in scripture where the Holy Spirit is given to people through the laying on of hands, and it references the same occurring with prophetic gifts in 1 Timothy 4:14 where it states, "Do not neglect your gift, which was given you through prophecy when the body of elders laid their hands on you." We have the ability to give to whomever we choose, whenever we choose. Certainly it is not always *wise* to do so, and in Chapter 10 we will discuss some issues that can arise when indiscriminately laying hands on people, but as a whole we have both the ability and the right to help accelerate the spiritual growth of others through impartation. It doesn't require a special writ from God any more than healing the sick does (which, if you didn't already know, we are encouraged to heal the sick freely in Christ). God actually *wants* us to steward our gifts with maturity instead of asking Him for permission every time we turn around. It's the difference between the relationships of an adult and a child versus an older adult and his full-grown son. In the latter example the two men might choose to do something together but the mature adult son isn't going to constantly ask his father for permission because he has grown in wisdom, discernment, understanding, and maturity and knows how to wisely utilize that which he is responsible for, while in the former example the child would lack all of these things and still need to get permission from his father.

I believe that impartation prayer is a method God has given us to strategically accelerate spiritual growth for ourselves and others. However, it works best when we are active participants. In my own life, I have made it a point to intentionally cultivate both my relationship with God and a strong prayer life, and while that has evolved in many ways over time, I believe that nothing is a substitute for intentional time alone with God. In the end, anyone can get prayed for and anyone can impart one to another, but those who are intentional to steward the gifts are those who will receive the most benefit and have the most to share with others long-term.

Chapter 4

Spiritual Math

One of the beliefs I have about the spiritual world around us is that it is far more mathematical than we realize. In the natural we can see evidence of fractals (repeating numerical patterns) in snowflakes, tree roots and branches, and even the veins on leaves. We see hexagons in beehives and turtle shells. We live on a planet that has a precise planetary rotational speed with a moon that has a precise rotational speed that orbits it. Our planet is in a galaxy with other planets which each have a specific and definable orbit around the sun—which in itself is also in orbit through the galaxy. Each of these things are organized and mathematical in nature and can be measured and defined in some way through numbers. While numbers themselves are a concept, what they reveal about creation is a measurable, ordered system. I have come to believe that the spirit realm is very similar, and as a result this mathematical influence plays a significant role when it comes to the subject of impartation. In this chapter we are going to look at what the Bible says about spiritual math and its relationship to answered prayer and explore in some depth on the math of impartation.

One time, a few years ago, I had a brief conversation with an angel at the end of my driveway and he explained to me that everything in the spirit is measurable, but the problem we humans face is that we lack the ability to measure spiritual things. When he said this to me, what came to mind was the anime series *Dragonball Z* and the energy-level readers the characters used—a technology that literally allowed them to measure people's spiritual power. How convenient would it be if we could just pull out a device and quantify stuff like that? I think it could be pretty cool although it could also be badly misused. What this angel said to me was something I have pondered before, and it makes sense to me as I think about various scriptures. For example, when the angel in Daniel 10 was opposed by the Prince of Persia, why did Michael come to help instead of another divine messenger? Clearly someone knew how to identify who or what would be needed to carry that angel through the battle and successfully deliver the message to Daniel, which is why Michael showed up.

Military engagements, even in the spirit, aren't done at random. They use information to know an enemy's strengths and weaknesses and how much force will be required to overcome the foe. Even if we assume that angels and demons weren't measuring each other's levels of spiritual power through some kind of device, Michael still had to have some way of identifying the amount of strength that demonic prince possessed in order to know his personal intervention was required. What this means is that the angelic host have some means of identifying the level of spiritual power, strength, or ability that others possess, whether friend or foe, and they use this to wage war in the heavens against our enemies.

There are other verses that even more clearly express this idea of measurable mathematics in the spirit, and one pair of verses actually give us visible imagery of this process in regards to answered prayer. The apostle Paul once wrote, "Now to him who is able to do immeasurably more than all we ask or imagine, according to His power that is at work within us . . ." (Ephesians 3:20). I find this passage fascinating because Paul didn't just say that God could do anything—he first made a statement of measurement, that God is able to do things we cannot measure—which suggests that there are many other things that *can* be. Second, Paul made a conditional statement that it was *according to the power at work within us.* Now, if I suspected before reading this that one could measure energy levels in the spirit, this only further supports the idea. There is something about the level of power at work within us that influences what God will do in the earth. Not only that, but we can see in 2 Corinthians 3:18 something that suggests that we don't just grow in power, but do so in levels. It says, "And we all . . . are being transformed into his image with ever-increasing glory, which comes from the Lord, who is the Spirit." That phrase "ever-increasing glory" could also be written as "from one level of glory to another." Glory actually has measurable levels in that we can increase from one level to another— enough so that those levels are defined in some way in the spirit. If they weren't then they wouldn't be called "levels."

There are other passages in the Bible that directly speak to this concept of spiritual measurements and are often closely linked with faith. Romans 12 has something interesting to say about the subject, "For I say, through the grace given to me, to everyone who is among you, not to think of himself more highly than he ought to think, but to think soberly, as God has dealt to each one a measure of faith" (Romans 12:3, NKJV). That term "measure of faith" in this passage is the words *metron pistis* (which literally means "measure of faith"). What is fascinating is that if we look at the definition of the word *metron,* it is a mathematical term used to determine portions, distances, and quantities—a term of measurement (Strong). In Biblical times it would be used as a measuring rod (meter) as well as a vessel to portion wet or dry goods. It is the same word used in Luke 6:38 which says, "Give, and it will be given to you. A good measure, pressed down, shaken together and running over, will be poured into your lap. For with the measure you use, it will be measured to you" (NKJV). These aren't the only places that talk about quantities related to spiritual things. Ephesians 4:7 says, "But to each one of us grace was given according to the measure of Christ's gift" (NKJV), yet again using the same word *metron* to describe that a specific quantity of grace, a spiritual substance, was apportioned out to each one of us. When we look at what the Bible says about spiritual substances such as faith and grace in the above verses, it paints a far more mathematical picture about spiritual reality than we are used to. What are the implications of this, and how should we make use of it in our lives?

In my writings I often explain that faith is a spiritual force or energy that "gets things done" in the spirit—the power to accomplish things and alter reality. We could think of faith as almost being a kind of currency. If we want a certain result, we expend a certain level or amount of faith and the result is ours. In some ways, we are kind of "buying" an outcome in prayer as we release faith for it. I think that is sometimes why it is through both faith *and* patience that we inherit the promises of God[2]. Even if we lack sufficient faith initially, as we continue to pray and believe for something over time, we are engaging in an ongoing transaction to reach the required quantity of spiritual power needed to complete our answer to prayer. It's sort of like a spiritual layaway program for accessing the promises of God. Keep in mind that this talk about spending faith or spiritual power as a currency only works and/or makes sense if faith is quantifiable. While we cannot quantify it in the physical realm at this time, I suspect that angels actually can and do measure our faith when it comes time to put things into action.

Revelation 5 and 8 shed some light on how framing in prayer works, something that allows us to target our prayers, so we are going

---

[2] Hebrews 6:12

to look at the verses and then I will break down how we can put this principle into practical use in prayer:

And when he had taken it, the four living creatures and the twenty-four elders fell down before the Lamb. Each one had a harp and they were holding golden bowls full of incense, which are the prayers of God's people (Revelation 5:8).

Another angel, who had a golden censer, came and stood at the altar. He was given much incense to offer, with the prayers of all God's people, on the golden altar in front of the throne. The smoke of the incense, together with the prayers of God's people, went up before God from the angel's hand. Then the angel took the censer, filled it with fire from the altar, and hurled it on the earth; and there came peals of thunder, rumblings, flashes of lightning and an earthquake (Revelation 8:3-5).

Revelation 5:8 speaks of the prayers of the saints as being collected in golden bowls. In Revelation 8 those prayers are referred to as incense, and that incense made up of prayers is combined with the fire of God then thrown back down onto the earth. In that passage, the end result of filling the bowls are that answers to our prayers get sent back to the earth—potentially with earth-shaking changes. Each bowl has a defined size, which we know because it is possible to fill them. If something can be filled, then it has a quantity associated with it—which means prayer can in some way be quantified. The fact that the Bible shows us our prayers are measured aligns with what I am suggesting here—that spiritual power is quantifiable and that we have been given both wisdom and ability to make use of that to further our own spiritual growth and advance the Kingdom of God in the earth.

To use this knowledge to "frame" a prayer, we simply have to define more specifically in our mind what we are praying for. All of our prayers go toward filling a bowl in heaven somewhere, and if a bowl doesn't exist for that thing prior to us praying, then our prayer creates one. Thus, if we are specific with our prayers and expectations, we can create a prayer bowl that matches more specifically what we seek, and that can influence the speed at which that bowl is filled.

The primary reason for growing in spiritual power for a follower of Jesus is to perform the signs, wonders, and miracles, divine healing, prophetic encouragement, words of knowledge, and more that Jesus taught his original disciples to do. It is to help us cast out demons and set captives free at a faster rate and with significantly greater ease. And while there are those who use these principles improperly and lord their spiritual influence over others, Jesus taught that those who were the greatest in the Kingdom were to become the servants of all.[3] Paul taught that ". . . we have this treasure in earthen vessels, so that the surpassing greatness of the power will be of God and not from ourselves . . ." (2 Corinthians 4:7). Later in that same letter (Chapters 11 and 12) he berated what he referred to as "super-apostles" for lording their positions over others and boasting in their great deeds. Growing in spiritual power doesn't negate the need to grow in the fruit of the spirit, but poor character also doesn't negate the need to grow in spiritual power.

I want us to really consider the implications of the idea that our prayers are measured in units of spiritual power. If we look at things from a perspective of quantifiable spirituality, a number of different contributing factors all tie in to answered prayer. The level of faith

[3] Matthew 23:11

we each have is going to convert to a certain amount of spiritual power released each time we pray, and the more we pray the faster the heavenly bowls get filled. If we pray in agreement with others there is a synergistic effect[4] which releases an increased quantity of power as well. When we put these and other power-releasing activities together, we will find that the speed at which we fill prayer bowls and see prayers answered accelerates.

I get that this sounds incredibly work-based, as though we only receive from God based on our own effort, but there are verses that suggest this is one part of how prayers truly do get answered. Any time we pray, we release spiritual power to change reality, and evidence of this transactionality is visible throughout scripture. Amos 3:7 says, "Surely the Sovereign Lord does nothing without revealing his plan to his servants the prophets" which suggests that we have a vital part to play in the partnership between heaven and earth, and releasing spiritual power through faith and prayer is part of that role. On the other hand, we live under grace, and while there is a transactional partnership between us and heaven, Jesus is also our Chief Intercessor who sits at the right hand of God. The Bible says in Hebrews 7:25 that Jesus ". . . lives to make intercession . . ." and in Revelation 8, it shows us that our prayers get mixed with fire from the altar in heaven. Both of these point to the idea that we aren't doing this all alone and that Jesus helps us out (a *lot*), but it is still a partnership and our own spiritual power has a part to play. If that was all there was to the situation, we could simply do a bunch of math, figure out how much we need to pray, and we would get all of our prayers answered all the time, but it isn't that simple. We are in a spiritual battle and enemy forces oppose us. Sometimes the enemy hijacks our results even when a prayer bowl has been filled and the answer sent. This is one reason why we have to pray things through

---

[4] Deuteronomy 32:30; Matthew 18:19

to completion, remaining persistent until we see the answers manifest. There is always a response from Heaven to every prayer we pray, but sometimes that response is attacked by the enemy.

There are mathematical, measurable quantities of power needed to bring change onto the earth, and they are usually released through prayer. Like with the golden bowls, when the necessary amount of time had passed, the so-called "fullness of time,"[5] God moved. When we pray, we have the disadvantage of not knowing when these spiritual bowls have become full, but when they do, the answers we seek are sent to us. When we want to break through into something new, we may need to pray until that bowl is filled, and only then will we get our answer. When we understand the importance of releasing spiritual power, we will get more purposeful about both using and enhancing it.

Spiritual power is not the only quantifiable resource in the spirit—sin and righteousness work similarly. Genesis 15:16 has something interesting to say about this, stating, "In the fourth generation your descendants will come back here, for the sin of the Amorites has not yet reached its full measure." Yet again we see that things are being measured, just in this case it is sin or iniquity. In Romans 6:23 we see that "For the wages of sin is death . . ." which means that a certain amount of sin yields a specific amount of payment in death-wages. The corollary is that righteousness pays out in life-wages, but in both cases, something is being measured and a subsequent share apportioned.

We see this scripturally with impartation as well. Remember the conversation between Elijah and Elisha? As already mentioned in 2 Kings 2:9-10, Elisha asked to receive a double-portion of Elijah's spirit—and Elijah told him the conditions under which that would be possible. This means that *both prophets* recognized that one's spirit

---

[5] Galatians 4:4

could be measured by or divided into portions—yet another way in which we see spiritual things quantified.

While all of this may sound highly theoretical, what if I told you that someone has figured out real-life math associated with spiritual change? Author Gregg Braden explains in his book *The Divine Matrix* that it takes only the square root of 1% of a population to start the process of effecting positive change. This means that in a population of 1 million, it only takes 100 people to start influencing positive spiritual transformation (Braden, *The Divine Matrix, 115-116*). If we figure the world is increasing in population with a [rounded] population of 8 billion people then according to Gregg Braden's math, the approximate number of people required to internally hold that change in their hearts to begin to see positive external results in the world would be 8,945 people. Whether the result is reduced crime, increased financial wellness, or anything else, any more people than that simply accelerates the process. In this manner, the ripple effects of individual spiritual power have actually been quantified to some small degree.

If we look at all of the places in scripture where spiritual power and other non-tangibles such as sin, righteousness, faith, and prayer have been quantified, we will discover that our spiritual life is far more measurable than we have previously understood. Now that we understand there is a mathematical arrangement to our spiritual life, we can use it to accelerate our spiritual growth. In the next chapter we are going to look at how we can actively use this wisdom to pursue an increase in spiritual power, see an increase in answered prayer, and expand our spiritual influence.

Chapter 5

Pursuing Exponential Growth

In the previous chapters we discussed how impartation is mathematical in nature, how we can give spiritual power to others without losing it ourselves, and how impartation can function as a seed that we can cultivate to help us grow in spiritual power. Now we are going to look at how the power of impartation can be used to pursue exponential growth in spiritual power, which ultimately looks like more effective prayers and better results. While intentional impartation might not exactly mirror exponential growth, when used consistently in a group it has that potential, and regardless, it can help us to move in that direction at an expanded rate.

Ultimately, the goal behind growing in spiritual power is to increase effectiveness in administrating the Kingdom of God. This can look like different things on the surface, but it all can be distilled into some form of answered prayer. And who doesn't want their prayers answered faster and better? As we grow in spiritual power, we can expect to see an accelerated rate of change in the world around us as a direct result of expanding the flow of heaven's virtue in and through us. As discussed previously, this isn't about becoming someone well-known by man or developing importance by human standards, but by being transformed in spirit and body to manifest the mandate of heaven. It is not the same as having a personal relationship with the Father, Son, and Holy Spirit, nor is it a substitute for developing a lifestyle of intimacy with the Godhead.

Nothing in this book should be understood to be or taken as a substitute for a relationship with God, but instead is meant to show some ways we can shortcut the process of growing in spiritual power to influence our world.

IMPARTATION MATH

To understand how impartation functions in real life, we need to review a few basic principles—what I am going to refer to as the "rules" of impartation. While I am labeling them as such, they represent how impartation tends to function in most cases, but there are always outliers. Keep in mind any time something appears to break a rule it is because a different rule is acting upon it to cause the difference from normal values. We discussed some of these concepts in Chapter Three, but the key rules are as follows:

1) Impartation passes on a small percentage of spiritual virtue and/or a seed of a spiritual gift or ability.
2) If we have received it in our own lives, we can give it away.
3) If we impart to someone, what we give is refilled in us by the Holy Spirit unless . . .
4) We have not assimilated it before we share it. If we have not, we may give away that which we received and never truly own it.
5) If we have assimilated something into our life and we impart it, we do not lose ours but share additionally with others.

Now that we have covered the basic rules (as I understand them at present), we will look at an example of how this works using numbers and percentages I have arbitrarily assigned to represent how these rules tend to function. Presume that a person's normal spiritual power or virtue is valued in percentages as 100%. When he goes to pray over someone and pass on spiritual power, he will only share a small portion of it (which we will label as 1% for simple discussion but it could be higher, lower, or variable). If he imparts to 100 people, doing earthly math he would have no more spiritual virtue to pass on, but thankfully, in a normal situation we don't lose what we impart. Power flows through us much like a river that collects in a reservoir. When we impart to someone else, the reservoir level drops slightly but is soon refilled by the river still feeding it. Practically speaking this means there is a limitless supply of God-energy available to us in any and every situation. One of our goals is to enlarge our reservoir so more can flow through us in any moment.

The beauty of this ability is that without anyone doing extra "work," we can intentionally expand one another's operation in kingdom power simply by sharing what we have received. Because we only receive a small portion, it often takes a moderate amount of impartation and other spiritual growth over time before we notice significant changes. However, it is important to realize that while receiving impartation from many people and/or many times can be helpful, it is not some magical process by which we can force God into doing things our way and on our timetable. Receiving prayer from a thousand people with no actual engagement of what we received accomplishes little to nothing, and I have witnessed this happen for people I know. This doesn't mean impartation is useless, but rather we must understand how to make this impartation effective and engage it for it to demonstrate much effect. More is not always better, having much to do with how we steward what we have been given. Collecting five gallons of water with a sieve will yield less benefit than collecting a single cup of water. It's about gathering, maintaining, and growing, not going through the motions of collecting for the sake of collecting—we're not spiritual hoarders.

We are going to discuss Elijah and Elisha again in this chapter, so we will read that scripture passage once more. 2 Kings 2:9-10 says:

> When they had crossed, Elijah said to Elisha, "Tell me, what can I do for you before I am taken from you?"
>
> "Let me inherit a double portion of your spirit," Elisha replied.
>
> "You have asked a difficult thing," Elijah said, "yet if you see me when I am taken from you, it will be yours—otherwise, it will not."

Most people look at this passage and think that Elisha was asking for double the quantity of spiritual power and prophetic capacity that Elijah operated in, but that's not what happened. In historical Jewish culture, inheritance rules meant that the firstborn son received what is called a *double portion*. For example, if a father had four sons, he would divide his inheritance into five portions; the eldest son would get two portions and the other three sons would each get a single portion. Elisha wasn't asking for twice what Elijah had—he was requesting to receive the two portions of inheritance that a firstborn son would receive from his father. In fact, we see this reflected a few verses later when he watches Elijah taken up to heaven in a whirlwind. It says, "Elisha saw this and cried out, 'My father! My father! The chariots and horsemen of Israel!'" (2 Kings 2:12), confirming that he did indeed recognize Elijah as his father and he had become the prophet's son. While I think most people want to receive the "double portion" from others, I'm not actually clear on how easy that is to pass on to others. However, whether we are able to readily pass on double portions or not, we can be assured that we can always impart *something*.

Going back to the math analogy. Consider that when imparting, we give someone 1% of the spiritual power or spiritual gifts we possess (remember this is an arbitrary value used to represent a small amount). Using those numbers, if a person receives impartation of 1% of their total power 100 times, then that individual's spiritual capacity would essentially double. While there is no limit to the amount of virtue we can receive or give, if we can only transfer 1% at a time it will take a while to notice any effects. Ultimately, the goal is to enlarge our reservoir of spiritual power so more can flow through us in any moment. This means that the speed at which we see divine healing, deliverance, and much more should see an increase over time, and really the same will occur for answered prayer as a whole. Additionally, as our reservoir enlarges, we are able to impart more virtue to others when we pray as well. For example, even if the percentage we impart remains the same, as we enlarge our reservoir we become able to release a greater amount to others. In physical terms, 1% of 100 gallons is far less than 1% of 100,000 gallons and our spirits work similarly.

If we want to see this occur on a wider scale, we would have to become more intentional about it. As we discussed in the previous chapter, we have to not just receive impartation but we have to do something to assimilate it and truly make it become a part of us. Hopefully we aren't solely relying on this to grow and are using what we receive to minister to those around us.

Exponential Growth

Exponential growth is growth that increases in speed-of-growth over time. A good example is a farmer and his crops. When a farmer plants a single plant, it produces seeds—not one, but many seeds per plant. For simplicity let us say one plant produces 20 seeds. If a farmer plants those seeds and each seed bears fruit, he will harvest 400 seeds. If he plants those seeds and they all bear fruit at the next harvest, he will harvest 8,000 seeds. Repeated continuously it will then be 160,000 seeds, then 3.2 million, then 64 million, and so on. At some point he will be unable to plant all of the seeds he would theoretically obtain due to exponential growth over time. What we are going to do is apply the concept of exponential growth to the principles behind impartation.

As we discussed previously, Impartation Math shows us how we can impart a small portion of our spiritual ability to others as a seed that can be cultivated and grown. But what if we didn't just do this randomly and occasionally? What if instead, a group of people caught the vision for how to grow intentionally and regularly put these principles into practice? Let's look at that now.

Imagine that a group of five people met every week for prayer and/or ministry of some kind. Then imagine that each time they met, they prayed for one another to receive impartation from the measure of the Holy Spirit on their lives. To explain this (and stay consistent for us math nerds), I am using the following math rules, which are simply meant to demonstrate how this principle functions and are not an exact formula for impartation math:

1) When one prays for another, roughly 1% of their total spiritual force is imparted (1% representing a small amount/in seed form)
2) When that impartation is assimilated, the total spiritual power increases to make a new total.
3) It is assumed everyone assimilates all they receive.
4) Everyone in the group starts at 100 spiritual power (SP).

If at the first meeting everyone imparts 1% to everyone else (1 SP), at the end of the meeting everyone is now at 104 points of SP. At the next gathering, everyone gives 1.04 SP away so each person goes away with 108.16 SP. By the end of 10 meetings, each person would be at approximately 148 SP, nearly 1.5 times what they began with. If this continued weekly for six months, he or she would have at least 277 SP, almost 3 times the starting point. Now, while these numbers are only a rough representation of how this works and not literal measurements of spiritual power, they reflect the spiritual mathematics that occur when we engage in spiritual transactions of any kind, and when we are aware of this, we can make purposeful use of these principles in our lives—intentionally and regularly imparting one to another to accelerate our growth rate of spiritual power.

Keep in mind that this example reflects growing in spiritual power *only* through impartation and not through any other means, which is unrealistic. In truth, everyone who is actively engaged in their spiritual journey will gradually grow in spiritual power over time anyway, though often slowly, and this would only enhance the results in the above scenario. Now imagine what could happen if this group continued to do their weekly meetings regularly for years with people coming and going, picking up the benefits of both giving and receiving in impartation culture, carrying it with them to other places, and with the initial group continuing to grow both in number and in power over time. Imagine if instead of five people the group had twenty or fifty, and that in addition to regular impartation, they spent time in corporate worship and intercession for their group, the region, and more. Their spiritual power levels would naturally increase into the thousands and even tens of thousands—and while we still don't know quite what that would look like, hundreds of times their initial starting point would *have* to yield noticeable results. What if this was a God-designed way that we could help one another make leaps and bounds forward in our ability to see our prayers answered, miracles released, our communities transformed, and experience the manifestation of the Kingdom on earth as it is in heaven? I believe it is.

Personally, I have experienced the benefits of accelerating spiritual growth through intentional focus. I think that sometimes people can confuse the idea that we get everything in the Kingdom as a free inheritance in seed form with the idea that we get it for free at full maturity. Jesus told a parable about the mustard seed of faith in Mark 4:30-32, saying:

> Again he said, "What shall we say the kingdom of God is like, or what parable shall we use to describe it? It is like a mustard seed, which is the smallest of all seeds on earth. Yet when planted, it grows and becomes the largest of all garden plants, with such big branches that the birds can perch in its shade."

The point of this parable wasn't about just needing to have a seed—it was that as the seed grew, the increasing benefits would be revealed. I believe that impartation is essentially a means of both planting new seeds and watering the seeds we have already received from Heaven. The more intentional we are about it, the more watering the plants get, and with better nurture comes better and faster growth. Jesus wasn't teaching his disciples to rest and do nothing. He was trying to explain how growth over time would release increasing benefits, and that as we purpose towards that, other people will be able to benefit from the power of God working through our lives. Intentional impartation is one way we can help maximize this growth with one another.

Chapter 6

Sowing and Reaping

One of the things people want to know is how they can grow in spiritual power when impartation isn't readily available from others. While there are many ways to grow, such as through worship, soaking prayer, and directly praying for God to increase our power level, this book is targeted toward impartation—so that is where we will focus. Even if we don't have others readily laying hands on us, we can still receive benefits over time as a result of imparting to others as a result of the Law of Sowing and Reaping, which we briefly discussed in the first chapter.

There are two primary verses that can be used to explain the Law of Sowing and Reaping in scripture. The first is Luke 6:37-38 which says,

> Do not judge, and you will not be judged. Do not condemn, and you will not be condemned. Forgive, and you will be forgiven. Give, and it will be given to you. A good measure, pressed down, shaken together and running over, will be poured into your lap. For with the measure you use, it will be measured to you.

This verse has a lot of detail but the underlying message is quite simple—what we put out, we get back, whether it is judgments, condemnation, forgiveness, spiritual power, or anything else.

Furthermore, when we sow it out we receive it back in a greater degree than our output. The passage presents wisdom about what and how we act and think because "with the measure you use, it will be measured to you." The second passage that expresses this concept is Galatians 6:7-9 which states:

> "Do not be deceived: God cannot be mocked. A man reaps what he sows. Whoever sows to please their flesh, from the flesh will reap destruction; whoever sows to please the Spirit, from the Spirit will reap eternal life. Let us not become weary in doing good, for at the proper time we will reap a harvest if we do not give up."

This passage shows us another aspect of this Law—that it makes a mockery of God to think we can sow without reaping, because whatever we sow, we are guaranteed to reap. Galatians 6 has two tidbits of wisdom for us in this regard. The first is to pay attention to what we sow because everything either brings death or life with it in return. The second nugget of wisdom is that we must persevere in our sowing because while things do not always appear immediately, as long as we persist we *will* receive our harvest. Hebrews 6:12 explains the concept by saying, "We do not want you to become lazy, but to imitate those who through faith and patience inherit what has been promised." Faith and patience are primary keys to reaping what we have sown.

Both of the passages above show us that whatever we put out, and in the measure which we put it out, we will receive a return in like kind. Examples in the natural would be if we plant corn, we will grow corn stalks and if we plant acorns, we will grow oak trees—and the law works the same way for spiritual things. What this means for answered prayer is that if we want to accelerate our growth in spiritual power, we can intentionally sow in order to intentionally reap. One important point to remember about utilizing this law is that it is effective, but rarely quick. Think about it—when someone plants a seed, it takes weeks to months for it to grow and sometimes years before it produces edible fruit. However, there is a prophetic promise in scripture that points to a time where we will be able to immediately reap the fruit of the good seeds we have sown. Amos 9:13a says, "'The days are coming,' declares the Lord, "when the reaper will be overtaken by the plowman—and the planter by the one treading grapes. . .'" In normal life, it is impossible to harvest barely moments after a seed is sown or for someone to harvest and crush grapes minutes after the new vines are planted, but God has promised we will be able to experience this. I believe that even while we are using the normal process of sowing and reaping, we can believe to experience instantaneous returns.

I want to share a vision the Lord gave me roughly 15 years ago that relates to how the Law of Sowing and Reaping is useful for growing in spiritual power. Back in 2004 to 2006 I lived in State College, PA, and some friends and I used to hold a six-hour prayer vigil at my church every other Friday night using Mahesh Chavda's *Watch of the Lord* format. During one Watch, I was asking God why not much spiritual change was taking place in our church. To the four of us, the Sunday services were noticeably different on the weeks we prayed versus the weeks we didn't. We all recognized this and as a result began to hold the prayer meetings weekly. With the change we made, we all expected far more than we saw taking place. Personally, in my immaturity it felt like our prayers just weren't doing much good and I was a bit disappointed. I realize now that it was presumptuous and somewhat naïve of me to question whether our prayers were being answered since God responds to every single prayer we pray. I was looking at what I could observe externally, not taking into account that God often works on things which are not visible, such as transforming the hearts of those in our congregation. With that said, as a group we expected supernatural displays of power such as healings and miracles, and as we discussed this one night, I discovered that we *all* felt some disappointment. Our team didn't sense much spiritual momentum as a church in spite of the consistent intercession from us and other members and in response to this, God gave me a vision.

I saw a faerie man, much like a leprechaun cobbler, sitting at a wooden bench tapping away at something with tools. I couldn't see what he was doing, but as he did so he produced this sparkling red dust. I watched him making this glitter-like dust and also saw an octagonal gemstone of the same ruby hue sitting on the table near him. The facets of the gem were divided into eight sections, almost like pieces of a pie, and five of them were a glowing red while the other three sections remained dim. As the faerie tapped at his table and made this red dust, one of the dim red slices became a glowing red as I watched another octagonal facet of the stone power up.

In this vision the faerie then walked throughout the church sanctuary, spreading the dust he had made on the pews, aisles, stage, etc. I then saw people sit in the pews on a Sunday morning, passively absorb the power contained in the ruby dust, then leave church for the week with no notable life change. During the week this faerie would return to work, producing this ruby glitter and sowing it in the church building on the weekends. When the final facet of the octagonal gem began to glow, it became evident in the vision that the faerie had reached a new level of spiritual power. The dust he now produced was larger in size and brighter in color even though he put the same amount of time and energy into it each week as he had before. When he spread it around the sanctuary, people absorbed not just enough to maintain where they were, but enough that they began to change and grow in their spirituality.

This vision was profound to me then and remains so even today. It clearly demonstrated that as we obtain new levels in the spirit, we have a greater capacity to cause change in the lives of those around us. In the vision, the faerie represented me, but also our entire intercessory team, and the red dust was the power of God. What this vision showed me was that as we engaged in our spiritual disciplines throughout the week, then gathered together on weekends for prayer, we were releasing God's power throughout the sanctuary. As we continued to do this faithfully, two things would happen: First, we would individually break through into new levels in the Spirit. Second, everyone else would step into new levels of breakthrough as well. Our forward momentum would push others forward as well, and as more people stepped into greater freedom, it could accelerate even further. The personal message for me was that while I could not control or influence anyone else's ability to engage the Holy Spirit and the power of God on deeper levels, as I chose to discipline myself to walk in greater fruitfulness, it would naturally cause those around me to reap the benefits as well.

The thing about sowing and reaping is that it functions like all spiritual laws—and in reality, all natural laws too. Laws are impartial. They don't pick and choose who they want to work for or how they will function. They operate the same way each and every time, and the only time we get different results is if additional influences (usually other laws) act upon the situation. Whatever we sow, we will reap. This can be quite useful as a tool for accelerating personal spiritual growth and is especially helpful for those who do not have people around them pouring impartation into them. According to the Law of Sowing and Reaping, we are guaranteed that if we pour into others, we will receive back in kind. Proverbs 11:25

demonstrates this concept, saying, "A generous person will prosper; whoever refreshes others will be refreshed." In other words, if someone wants to live in prosperity, if they give to others then they will receive prosperity as well. If someone wants to be refreshed, go and bring refreshing to others and it will come to us too. Likewise, if we want to receive impartation then we should go impart to others. If we want to increase in spiritual power, we should release it through prayer and we will receive an increase in our lives as well. Many years ago the Lord told me that if I wanted to get better at healing the sick through healing prayer then one of my options was to pray for a ton of sick people and by sowing healing power, I would reap an increase in that same healing virtue and would improve my effectiveness in healing the sick. The same concept applies to growing in any aspect of spiritual power, and if we use this method consistently then while it may take time to pay dividends back to us, we can trust that it *will* pay out and we *will* experience the increase.

This could be seen as a form of spiritual training, and I want to share a story and discuss the concept of spiritual training as it relates to sowing and reaping. I have shared this story in other books of mine as well. One of the keys to any effective exercise program is that of exhaustion. Regardless of the means of exercise, whether swimming, running, lifting weights, or anything else, the goal is to work muscles to a breaking point, rest and recover, and do it again. Each time one does this, the muscles will grow stronger as they repair. A little-known secret is that we can do the same with our spirits—something I discovered by accident during another one of our Watch meetings.

The evening before the 2004 Presidential Elections, a Monday night, I felt led to have an all-night personal prayer vigil, and in doing so spent over twelve hours praying for God's hand to lead and guide both the elections and the nation. The last three hours of the morning, from about 3-6 am, I was joined by Diane and Jerry, my two primary Watch partners. That Friday night we held the Watch as we normally did, but this time something unique happened to me. Shortly into the night I felt completely spiritually drained. I had no internal compulsion or energy to pray, worship, or engage in any way at all. I was totally tapped out and had nothing to give (which is abnormal for me), so I just laid on the floor on my back, resting in God's presence. I don't recall if worship music was on at the time or not, but Diane was waving a flag and as she walked over and waved it over me, she was saying the word "fire," praying for God's fire to fall upon me. I remember that at one moment I observed how drained I felt, the next moment I looked up at her waving her flag, then another second later I looked down again and in that brief instant the Lord had renewed my spirit—I went from spiritually empty to spiritually full in the blink of an eye!

As I pondered this later, I realized that my spirit was used to me praying for six hours every *other* week, but not twelve hours at the beginning of a week and another six on the weekend. Compared to physical exercise, it would be like regularly running a mile every other day, but then one day deciding to run two miles in the morning and another mile that afternoon. In simple terms, I had overtaxed my spirit and I was wiped out. However, I never felt that level of tiredness again—even after Diane (who was also the leader of our prayer group) felt the Lord urging her to make the Watch a weekly event, and even though I began praying regularly on Monday nights for anywhere from five to nine hours as well. In the same way that an athlete trains to handle increased demand on the body, from that point on I was able to handle a greater measure of sustained spiritual activity due to exercising my spirit.

This is just one example of how sowing and reaping can function in our lives and lead to breakthrough into new levels in the spirit.

The Power of Impartation

While previously my spirit had trouble handling the level of spiritual output, I exhausted myself by sowing out in prayer, and the result of that was reaping a measure of spiritual growth in my ability to pray for extended periods of time. There are a variety of ways we can work this spiritual law for our benefit, and exhaustion is just one valid example. For those who want to grow in spiritual power, the Law of Sowing and Reaping is one helpful tool, and when we use it to impart to others we will find that we will receive benefits from it as well, accelerating our own growth.

Chapter 7

Apostolic Versus Prophetic Impartation

When it comes to impartation, there are two primary categories all impartation falls under. I learned this through a prophetic dream I had back in the summer of 2017 which seemed to suggest that when God has a message He wants people to carry, He sends two kinds of messengers. The first are apostolic messengers—those who have lived out the message, have struggled through the ups and downs as they have pioneered the experience, and who have become the living embodiment of that which they speak. The second is as a prophetic messenger, receiving the missive through revelation. Prophetic messages are often those given by the forerunners, as they are speaking of spiritual realities that have not yet manifested. Neither means of carrying a message is better than the other, nor is either inferior to the other; they are simply different. Apostolic messengers carry the experiences within them while prophetic messengers are often speaking of new things—things they have yet to attain to but which God desires to release into the earth.

The same is true of impartation, and it is important to understand the difference between the two. Apostolic impartation is what we have been discussing thus far in this book and especially in the first chapter—where we impart something to someone out of the virtue that we possess in our lives. Think "active and working." Prophetic impartation is different. In theory we cannot give something to others that we do not have, but prophetic impartation uses the power of decrees to release things from Heaven directly to another person. We act as a catalyst but ultimately the impartation bypasses us entirely. For this kind of impartation, think "the power of decree."

The idea of passing something on that isn't actively at work in our lives sounds strange at first, but we actually do this in normal life regularly. For example, many people teach things they haven't done and we consider it perfectly reasonable. Science teachers teach about volcanoes, water currents, outer space, atoms and subatomic particles, cellular respiration, and all sorts of other natural phenomenon and physiological processes they have never personally witnessed or studied on-site. History professors teach about long-dead cultures they have never personally encountered. People teach business courses all the time who have no actual experience running a business. It is actually quite common in higher education to do exactly that, and it happens in the Church as well.

End-times prophecy is a perfect example of this. We have well-known speakers, authors, and teachers who have deep understanding of their subject matter, but at the end of the day it is essentially educated conjecture considering not a single one of them has ever actually "experienced" the futuristic end times they are speaking about. People flock to conferences, buy books, and are glued to television programs with these individuals discussing theories that don't even necessarily influence our day-to-day lives, but those sharing that information are prophetic messengers of a sort—releasing something that is not actively working in their own lives and yet of which they have obtained some level of revelation, knowledge, and understanding of nonetheless. Prophetic impartation operates on this same principle.

Hebrews 11:1 states, "Now faith is the substance of things hoped for, the evidence of things not seen" (NKJV). Faith is the means by which we can pass on substances that are not tangible and have not actually become realized yet, and it is through faith that we can decree and establish things in other people's lives even if we aren't walking them out ourselves. How does that work? Hebrews 11 actually has a lot to say about this subject. Hebrews 11:3 says, "By faith we understand that the universe was formed at God's command, so that what is seen was not made out of what was visible." God commanded the universe to form, decreeing it into existence, and after He made the decree it was established. Job 22:28 states that we have this same ability stating, "You will also declare a thing, and it will be established for you . . ." (NKJV). The scriptures show us that we do not have to possess something to impart it to others so long as we declare it into existence through the authority and creative power God has already placed within us.

We see this power at work with the Old Testament Patriarchs as well. Hebrews 11:20-21 says, "By faith Isaac blessed Jacob and Esau in regard to their future. By faith Jacob, when he was dying, blessed each of Joseph's sons, and worshiped as he leaned on the top of his staff." The Law of Blessing is one example of prophetic impartation. Blessing is a creative ability whereupon we bestow life through our words. All throughout the Bible people blessed one another, and God blessed mankind. In the New Testament in Ephesians 1:3 we even have a promise that we can receive heavenly blessings in the spiritual realms. Likewise, we can bestow blessings upon ourselves and others through decrees.

Literally by saying things out loud, we can release things to other people even if we don't possess those abilities. We see this in Genesis 27:27 where Isaac blesses Jacob. It says, "And he came near and kissed him; and he smelled the smell of his clothing, and blessed him and said . . ." Note the last part where Isaac *said* something in order to bless him. When Esau came by for the blessing that should have been his, Isaac stated of Jacob, "I have blessed him—and indeed he shall be blessed . . ." (Genesis 27:33). Isaac was clear that through the power of his words he had released something into his son Jacob's life, and Isaac stated as much to confirm it was true.

The key benefit of this form of impartation is that it doesn't matter if no one in our sphere of influence is operating in a particular spiritual gift or virtue. We still have the ability to engage it by decree—whether over our own life or the lives of others. There are some people who don't have a community of people around them who can impart into their lives, and prophetic impartation, including the power of blessing, is a great way to get around that problem, offering yet another tool we can use to continue to accelerate the spiritual growth process in our lives and for those around us.

Chapter 8

Revelation as Impartation

In the previous chapter we discussed prophetic impartation, where we can give or receive something we do not have through the power of decree. Here we are going to look at something that is related in that it does not involve direct impartation from person to person, but is slightly different—receiving impartation directly from heaven through personal revelation.

Revelation is the supernatural release of wisdom, knowledge, or understanding about something—divine inspiration. It isn't just a new idea that helps us think about something differently—it causes literal change in our beliefs and understanding and may alter how we approach and respond to situations. When we receive revelation, there is an inner expansion that takes place—a quickening of our spirit. It is usually accompanied by a mental moment where an idea clicks into place. Oftentimes after receiving it, the revelation seems so obvious that we don't know why we didn't understand or realize that particular concept before.

Revelation typically comes to us in one of four ways:
1) Directly by download from the Holy Spirit without prompting stimuli.
2) Download from the Holy Spirit during a prompting stimuli such as reading, meditation, worship, etc.

3) Through listening to teachings by others (a very specific prompting stimulus).
4) Given to us by angelic messenger.

In reality, the Holy Spirit is the one who quickens all revelation within us, so regardless of the delivery method all of them are ultimately His work. Jesus spoke of the Holy Spirit's revelation-giving power in John 16:14 saying, "He will glorify me because it is from me that he will receive what he will make known to you." The exact manner in which we receive divine inspiration is not always that important. In other words, it doesn't matter if an angelic messenger delivers a missive or if we realize that same something while reading our Bible. What is most important is the internal transformation that occurs.

To be clear, information and revelation are not the same thing. I can listen to people talk about things I have never heard before, and as a result I will gain knowledge—new information. But something must take place on a spiritual level within me for that information to become revelation, and that is the key we are looking for. Why does it matter if something is inspired as opposed to learned? It comes down to impartation.

When we learn an idea, we have head knowledge. It is a mental construct that has no further ability or power beyond how we apply it with our minds and actions. With any form of divine inspiration, however, it carries virtue with it and creates inner transformation. In other words, when we receive revelation from heaven, we have in that moment received an impartation of something that makes changes in our soul and spirit. And, as we have discussed previously, once we receive something, we can give it away. Yet again, this is also a means by which we can receive impartation even if we are alone—as we engage the Holy Spirit He will reveal things to us, and as He reveals things to us they become implanted within our spirits and we can nurture that inspiration and let it grow and bear fruit.

In order to take advantage of this, it helps to understand how we can position ourselves to receive. Theoretically, receiving new revelation is not something we can make happen at will. By that I mean that if we were to decide right this moment that we wanted new revelation, it doesn't mean we will suddenly be struck with a heavenly download. All wisdom and knowledge is there for the taking, and desiring new revelation can certainly influence the speed at which we receive it—it's just not generally as fast as flipping a switch and turning a light on. Matthew 7:7-8 tells us, "Ask and it will be given to you; seek and you will find; knock and the door will be opened to you. For everyone who asks receives; the one who seeks finds; and to the one who knocks, the door will be opened." If we desire inspiration, we can look at that verse and trust that God will give us what we ask, but we must learn to be patient and go through the process.

One of the keys to receiving revelation is remaining open. When we close our hearts off to new ideas, we minimize the creative flow in our lives and stifle the power of the Holy Spirit. After all, when we receive divine inspiration it is things we *did not know before*, so we should expect it to be different than what we already understand and have experienced.

Another key is to find and listen to revelatory teaching. While that is kind of a broad suggestion, as what will be revelatory to one may not be to another, when we listen to or read teachings from someone and we experience that energy of revelation, we should consider connecting with more of their teaching material until we stop getting that sense of internal growth. When I listen to revelatory audio teachings, I usually listen to them twice. The first time I receive the revelation and my spirit grows. The second time is to help me mentally process the knowledge so that I understand it better with my conscious mind and help the revelation sink deeper. This is important because receiving new revelation means I have the seed of change within me, but more often than not it takes time to fully manifest. In some cases I may listen to it several times to deeply root within me what God is revealing.

As I mentioned previously, impartation often manifests in seed form—starting small and growing with time and tending. Pastor Peter Tan in his free eBook *The Spiritual World* has the following to say on this matter:

> The reason why it takes time for the outward manifestation of an inward reception and impartation is because the inward transformation is incomplete. Even though sometimes individuals think (mentally), and convince themselves that they already have it, in their true selves, they haven't got it fully until it is an automatic, subconscious and habitual part of their daily lives. . . . When one first receives a truth or a new impartation and understanding of life, they do not have it until it is within their subconscious, in their actions and is a part of their daily habit of life. It is not just when we think and believe about something that we have it, but it is when we are practicing the truth that we truly have it. It is when we are not thinking about it and yet it forms part of our substance of life-consciousness that we truly have absorbed it into us. (38-39)

Another way of receiving revelation, and thus increasing the potential to receive impartation accordingly, is by teaching or communicating to others. When a group of people engage an idea their understanding of it grows, but at times that group engagement also causes a pull on the prophetic, resulting in the teacher saying things he or she has never learned before. In other words, the teaching process itself uncovers new revelation, and sometimes the speaker is as surprised as everyone else! The times that has happened to me I have inadvertently paused as I take a moment and let my own brain absorb what I just said. In a more interactive teaching setting, a student may have just asked a question which the teacher is trying to answer, and as the teacher is answering, the new revelation comes forth. This is a manifestation of the gift of teaching, and the Holy Spirit is gracious to answer the student's question even if the teacher didn't know the answer in advance. That doesn't mean we need to find people to teach in hopes it will help us learn, but it is still a valid means by which revelation comes as we corporately pull on the revelatory flow of heaven.

Likewise, as an author and speaker, whether writing books, crafting articles for my website, or pondering what messages I want to share, they all cause revelation to slowly filter my way. When starting to write a book I might not understand everything I need to complete it, but frequently I end up adding multiple chapters to a book based off revelatory downloads during the writing process. In fact, the initial outline for this book only had nine chapters, not twelve, and the following chapter on Mantles was largely the result of revelation I received while intentionally discussing the subject with my wife in order to pull on revelation to write more fully on the subject. Being intentional with life circumstances as a means of pulling on revelation is a very real and often practical tool. Part of why this works is what I refer to as the Law of Focus, a subset of the Law of Sowing and Reaping. This spiritual law basically states that whatever I focus on and engage, I attract to me. I do also study the Bible and relevant material from others, but even as I ponder and study a subject, I receive revelation as new ideas come to me.

Sometimes when I study, I gain profound new understanding as my research turns into an interactive revelatory flow between the Holy Spirit and me.

As mentioned before, all information is accessible in the spirit and anyone who knows how to can gain inspiratory knowledge by wanting to. However, multiple factors influence how easily we do or do not receive that revelation. If we want to engage that prophetic flow, we should do things that position us under the spout where the revelation comes out. Prayer and fasting are tools we can use to help position ourselves, as is surrounding ourselves with others who are headed in the same direction. However, at the end of the day much of this still functions off the Law of Focus.

While not everyone is an author, teacher, or speaker, we can all make use of simple tools to engage the Law of Focus and activate the revelatory realm to receive a greater flow of inspiration and thus impartation. Journaling and discussion with others are two easy ways to do this. Another option is to talk to an empty room. I like to pace while I talk, and if I am on a long phone conversation with a friend, I can be found doing laps inside the house or wearing a hole in the grass in our yard. Talking to the air in order to practice, process, and pull on revelation is much the same, and I have been known to practice preaching messages in the same way. My wife says she always practices her teaching lessons aloud before she takes those lessons into the college classroom. Whether in public or private, a variety of different methods can help us actively engage the flow of revelation which in turn will enhance our spiritual growth.

Chapter 9

Mantles, Lampstands, and Spiritual Entities

One of the bigger Charismatic buzzwords is the term "mantle," and it's something that many believers seem to want to receive from every minister whose foot has ever graced a stage. Personally I think the term is widely misused and often mantles don't even function how most people think, but I believe they are related to the discussion on impartation so we are going to look at the concept here. I will attempt to explain how mantles appear to function from scripture, and then we can look at how and when it is appropriate to impart mantles from one person to another.

The primary function of a mantle is to provide or assist with spiritual authority (and thus provide further ability) to govern or steward an organization, whether a nation, a church, a business, or other group of people. The primary difference between an imparted spiritual gift and a mantle is that spiritual gifts come with a person and are resident within them whereas mantles come with a position and are not necessarily permanent to a person. Romans 11:29 tells us, ". . . for God's gifts and his call are irrevocable." One of the functions of a mantle is the ability to transfer something from one person to another in such a manner that the former no longer possesses it, and if mantles were a form of spiritual gift then this would be impossible. If they aren't spiritual gifts, how do mantles work?

Mantles are not something that reside within our spirits and do not become part of our innate being, but rather are placed upon us. This doesn't mean that they are undesirable, however, as a mantle is a bit like giving wings to a tiger—they can further elevate someone in an existing position or help establish someone in a newly created one. The best definition I have ever heard was from Kris Valloton, a senior leader at Bethel Church in Redding, California. I don't recall the name of his speaking message or I would include it for reference purposes, but it is the only explanation I have ever heard that truly not only makes sense in general but accounts for the difference between normal impartation and the passing on of mantles. In summary, Kris said that mantles go with the mission. An example of this would be the President of the United States (POTUS).

The US only ever has one lawful President at a time, so there is only one person able to occupy that position of authority. After the governing term is over and a new POTUS is elected, there is a day when the old POTUS steps down from the position and the new one assumes that authority. The position carries not just authority in the natural, but a measure of spiritual governing authority over the millions of citizens in the nation, and this is where mantles are involved. The one doing the governing is the one who needs it, not the one who used to be in that position. Theoretically, if a mantle were to remain with a former President then the new one would lack the spiritual authority needed to adequately govern the nation. Thus, whether they realize it or not, when one POTUS steps down and a new one is inaugurated there is a passing of the mantle from one to the other. In fact, the old President will never have use for that mantle again in his or her life—it would serve no purpose to keep the mantle for a position he will never occupy again. However, in certain circumstances, such as with massive and sweeping election fraud, it is entirely possible that a mantle does *not* get transferred, and in order for the unlawful ruler to obtain it he or she would have to basically steal it in the spirit—a subject we will address later in this chapter. This doesn't mean that an unlawful ruler automatically gets the mantle—it means that *if* they get the mantle, it will be through spiritual theft that matches their physical one.

We are going to look in more depth at how we can identify that mantles are tied to governing authority, but to do so we need to first understand where the terminology comes from. The term "mantle" as far as inheriting spiritual authority is concerned comes initially from the Elijah-Elisha inheritance story in 2 Kings. We have covered aspects of this story already, but this time we will look at a longer passage providing more context to get a better picture of what is going on. As necessary backstory, keep in mind that Elijah trekked around parts of Israel with Elisha in tow, heading from city to city before finally reaching the Jordan River. While there is prophetic significance to the places he stopped and the order he visited them, it has more to do with growing in the prophetic as a whole and less to do with impartation, so we will not cover that here. We are going to look at everything that happened from the time Elijah arrived at the river Jordan until Elisha crossed back over. Pay special attention to the verses where his cloak, or some translations say "mantle," comes into play. Second Kings 2:7-15 says:

Fifty men from the company of the prophets went and stood at a distance, facing the place where Elijah and Elisha had stopped at the Jordan. Elijah took his cloak, rolled it up and struck the water with it. The water divided to the right and to the left, and the two of them crossed over on dry ground.

When they had crossed, Elijah said to Elisha, "Tell me, what can I do for you before I am taken from you?"

"Let me inherit a double portion of your spirit," Elisha replied.

"You have asked a difficult thing," Elijah said, "yet if you see me when I am taken from you, it will be yours—otherwise, it will not."

As they were walking along and talking together, suddenly a chariot of fire and horses of fire appeared and separated the two of them, and Elijah went up to heaven in a whirlwind. Elisha saw this and cried out, "My father! My father! The chariots and horsemen of Israel!" And Elisha saw him no more. Then he took hold of his garment and tore it in two.

Elisha then picked up Elijah's cloak that had fallen from him and went back and stood on the bank of the Jordan. He took the cloak that had fallen from Elijah and struck the water with it. "Where now is the Lord, the God of Elijah?" he asked. When he struck the water, it divided to the right and to the left, and he crossed over.

The company of the prophets from Jericho, who were watching, said, "The spirit of Elijah is resting on Elisha." And they went to meet him and bowed to the ground before him.

This entire section is full of miracles and supernatural events, but let's hone in on the parts involving the cloak, or mantle, of Elijah. First, we see the prophet taking it, rolling it up (presumably to make a more rod-like shape), and then hitting the river with it to part the waters. Keep in mind this isn't a small stream—it is a river which would normally require some time and effort to cross without the supernatural part-the-waters method Elijah used. Furthermore, the newly uncovered riverbed they walked across was dry. Next, we see Elisha recognize Elijah as his spiritual father as the man is taken to heaven in a whirlwind, and this confirms to Elisha that, according to Elijah's promise, he receives the firstborn double-portion inheritance. Now, at some point Elijah must have either tossed his mantle down to the earth or it fell off him in the whirlwind because his protégé was able to pick it up and slap the river with it on the return trip in the same way they did on the first trek across.

While it isn't explicitly stated in the text, I suspect Elisha was testing something out when he did that. I personally believe Elisha used the cloak to hit the water not because the cloak itself was special, nor because he actually needed to use it, but because now that his mentor was gone he was thinking to himself "I really hope this works!" After all, someone who is faith-filled and fully convinced a miracle will happen doesn't say, "Where now is the Lord, the God of Elijah?" That's what someone who is incredibly hopeful, stepping out on a limb, and going for the fake-it-till-you-make-it method does. I can almost imagine him covering his eyes with one hand and hitting the river with the mantle in the other hand thinking "I'm going to look like a total idiot if this doesn't work." Keep in mind that the entire company of the sons of the prophets was staring at this entire process from the other side of the river so the pressure was on. Did he successfully inherit something from Elijah? Well, the water parted, which was a good sign, and then the rest of the prophetic company confirmed yet again that the spirit of Elijah rested upon Elisha—which in and of itself is an interesting choice of words. Don't get me wrong—I think that everyone who steps into new realms in operating in the supernatural goes through similar inner turmoil as Elisha must have, so I'm not making fun of him. I just think it is really interesting how even in this set of power-packed events we can see the man's humanity clearly shining through.

Now, this whole mantle-business ultimately comes out of this passage where we see a prophet, and in fact the *primary* prophet over Israel in that day, pass down his spiritual authority to his successor. I see this as being entirely separate from the double-portion impartation Elisha received from Elijah because the double portion was his inheritance as a son. The mantle was due to the position called "Prophet of Israel" he was to now occupy. If we look later in Elisha's life, we saw him attempt to mentor Gehazi, who eventually failed the test and was unable to inherit anything, but there *was* a position to fill and Elisha was unable to pass that mantle on to a new successor. Mind you, I'm not talking about the literal cloak of the prophet Elijah at this point but the spiritual authority that it represents prophetically in scripture.

We see this matter of passing mantles and even *dividing up* and *sharing* of mantles come up in a few other places in scripture. In 1 Samuel 24 there is an interesting encounter between King Saul and David. David had already been anointed as King by the prophet Samuel which had made Saul, the current king, jealous. After chasing some Philistines, Saul was out hunting for David and his group with the intent to kill him. While Saul is in a cave "relieving himself" (some translations say "covering his feet"— often a euphemism for having sex, not going to the bathroom), David sneaks into the cave and cuts a corner off of Saul's robe, and then later after the king exits the cave, David talks to him and attempts to demonstrate his innocence as far as kingdom-takeovers are concerned. While the encounter itself is generally just strange, I find it interesting that David has already been anointed as the new king and yet of all the things he could do in scripture, he cuts off a piece of cloth from the hem of Saul's mantle. While in the natural we can look at the idea that cutting up the king's clothing unnoticed meant that he could have killed Saul if he wanted to, yet I see a spiritual significance to the mantle-cutting act. Prophetically, in that moment, David laid additional claim to a portion of Saul's spiritual authority to rule the kingdom of Israel.

This isn't the only place we see the cutting up of a mantle. We see this happen again in 1 Kings 11 with Solomon and his descendants. 1 Kings 11:9-13 says:

> The Lord became angry with Solomon because his heart had turned away from the Lord, the God of Israel, who had appeared to him twice. Although he had forbidden Solomon to follow other gods, Solomon did not keep the Lord's command. So the Lord said to Solomon, "Since this is your attitude and you have not kept my covenant and my decrees, which I commanded you, I will most certainly tear the kingdom away from you and give it to one of your subordinates. Nevertheless, for the sake of David your father, I will not do it during your lifetime. I will tear it out of the hand of your son. Yet I will not tear the whole kingdom from him, but will give him one tribe for the sake of David my servant and for the sake of Jerusalem, which I have chosen."

While there is no mantle-ripping in this passage, it sets the stage for something that occurs later in that chapter. Solomon turns his back on God and serves demonic princes of other religions so God tells him that *most* of his kingdom will be taken from him. We go down just a bit later in the passage and Solomon is having issues with rebellions and insurrections, and one of them is led by Jeroboam, one of the king's officials. He is overseeing some kind of labor force, possibly building up defenses around Jerusalem (that part is unclear), when a prophet approaches him. The passage says:

About that time Jeroboam was going out of Jerusalem, and Ahijah the prophet of Shiloh met him on the way, wearing a new cloak. The two of them were alone out in the country, and Ahijah took hold of the new cloak he was wearing and tore it into twelve pieces. Then he said to Jeroboam, "Take ten pieces for yourself, for this is what the Lord, the God of Israel, says: 'See, I am going to tear the kingdom out of Solomon's hand and give you ten tribes. But for the sake of my servant David and the city of Jerusalem, which I have chosen out of all the tribes of Israel, he will have one tribe. I will do this because they have forsaken me and worshiped Ashtoreth the goddess of the Sidonians, Chemosh the god of the Moabites, and Molek the god of the Ammonites, and have not walked in obedience to me, nor done what is right in my eyes, nor kept my decrees and laws as David, Solomon's father, did. (1 Kings 11:29-33)

Jeroboam is working for Solomon overseeing a construction project and the prophet Ahijah approaches him and starts talking to him, apparently showing off some new clothes. When they are alone, Ahijah rips up his mantle as a prophetic act, hands ten pieces to Jeroboam to represent taking over ten of the twelve tribes of Israel, and keeps two pieces—one which represents the portion of the kingdom that will remain with Solomon's family and the other piece I honestly don't know what he did with because the text doesn't say. After Solomon dies, his son Rehoboam takes over, is even more of a tyrant than Solomon, and the kingdom revolts. The kingdom splits up and Jeroboam ends up with ten tribes of Israel and Rehoboam maintains control over Judah and the city of Jerusalem, all which Ahijah had prophesied would occur *when he split the mantle into pieces.*

The part we must note here related to mantles and spiritual authority is that Ahijah the prophet didn't just anoint Jeroboam to be king. He specifically and pointedly took hold of his mantle and ripped the cloth into pieces as a prophetic act to hand the ruling authority of ten of the twelve tribes of Israel over to Jeroboam.

These two examples of mantles being divided up, found with David and Jeroboam, are not the only places we see spiritual authority being divided or shared in some way. If we recall back in Numbers 11 with Moses, his governing authority was spiritually divided between himself and 72 elders of Israel as well. To recap, Numbers 11:16-17 says:

> The Lord said to Moses: "Bring me seventy of Israel's elders who are known to you as leaders and officials among the people. Have them come to the tent of meeting, that they may stand there with you. I will come down and speak with you there, and I will take some of the power of the Spirit that is on you and put it on them. They will share the burden of the people with you so that you will not have to carry it alone."

While I realize that God told Moses to bring seventy elders, there were two additional elders who were not present at the tent of meeting and yet the Holy Spirit fell upon them as well. The significance of this is that God recognized that Moses had too much going on, and instead of just telling him to mete out governing duties to the elders who were *already recognized* as elders among their people, God specifically had them attend the tent of meeting for a ceremony to transfer and share the spiritual authority upon Moses with the rest of them.

The Power of Impartation

If we contrast the encounter with Moses with those of David and Saul and with Jeroboam and Solomon/Rehoboam, we discover a few interesting details. First, we find that spiritual authority can be passed on prophetically even before it is transferred physically. Second, we discover that authority can be transferred even without the knowledge of the person who is actually in possession of that authority. I think that has interesting ramifications when it comes to who is in charge of a company, church, city, state, nation, or other governing body and that it is entirely within the realm of possibility to stage a spiritual coup long before a physical takeover ever occurs. Third, we see that authority can be passed on in a few different ways. It can be intentionally passed, such as when Elijah passed on his mantle to Elisha. It can be removed by force in the spirit, such as with David's situation with Saul. It can be forcefully shared or divided, such as with Jeroboam and Rehoboam and the kingdom-split, and finally, it can be intentionally shared, as with Moses and the elders of Israel. The Bible recognizes all of these as potential options when it comes to the passing on of spiritual authority, but I do think it is important to note one thing in particular.

Each time authority was forcefully transferred, it was done by God and not by man, even if a prophet was instructed to do so. The reason I say this is that this explanation is not meant as permission for people to do witchcraft in the spirit and basically attack a company, church, or governing municipality with spiritual takeover in mind. Forcefully taking or stealing a mantle is possible in the spirit, but unless God is the one doing the rearranging, it is wrong. While most readers aren't likely to want to do that anyway, I feel very strongly that I need to discuss this here. David didn't go hunting for a kingship, and neither did Jeroboam. Both men were approached by prophets of God (Baal and other spirits *also* had prophets) and neither man sought out a prophecy to decree them into a kingship position. There is nothing wrong with seeking out a promotion, but there are healthy ways to use spiritual principles to do it and there are unhealthy and evil ways to go about doing the same, and yet either means of going about it is likely to result in the promotion. Methods matter.

We see this symbolism of mantles representing authority in a few places in the New Testament as well. In Luke 15 Jesus tells the story of the prodigal son. After the son basically disowns his family and wastes his inheritance and then runs out of cash, he comes back to his dad hoping to get a servant's job. The father ignores the request and tells a servant to grab a robe, ring, and sandals for the son to put on, all of which symbolize his return to a position of authority as a son in the household. Now, the interesting thing about the robe is that it is basically the same as the various different words use in the Old Testament to describe mantles or cloaks, but written in Greek instead. In other words, the prodigal son gets not just a ring that signifies authority as a son over the material goods in the household, but the father gives him a mantle suggesting a return to spiritual authority as well.

In Matthew 21 we see the use of mantles yet again, but this time it is to herald the coming of Jesus, the Messiah, as he rides a donkey into Jerusalem. His disciples spread their cloaks on the donkey for Jesus to sit on, and then a huge crowd throw their cloaks across the roadway along with palm branches they cut as they start shouting out praises to Jesus. If we look at the fact that Jesus came to regain spiritual authority over the earth that Adam abdicated to Satan in the Garden of Eden, people casting their mantles down in front of him was a form of prophetic recognition of Jesus as their spiritual authority (even if in their minds they were expecting it in the natural as well).

LAMPSTANDS AND SPIRITUAL ENTITIES

Recognizing that it is possible to share or divide mantles then brings us to the question of how we can create them. In order to understand how to make a spiritual mantle, as well as how to properly understand how mantles relate to governing authority, I think it is also important to understand how an organization or group functions as a single entity in the spirit. I talk about this subject in my book *The Gamer's Guide to the Kingdom of God* in a chapter called *Guilds*, but I will attempt to explain the concept here using non-gaming lingo. One of the things that happens when any group of people get together with a specific cause, ideal, purpose, etc. in mind is that they essentially create a spiritual entity. This entity has the ability to grow in the spirit over time as people influence and contribute to it spiritually, it has the ability to carry blessings and curses, have angels assigned to it, and more. While it may not have intellect in the way we characterize a sentient being, it does seem to have the ability to connect with and influence the lives of its members, which we will explore shortly.

Before going further, I want us to look at some scriptures that shed some light on the subject. We see some important keys in the book of Revelation that require a little unpacking. John the Revelator was taken into a series of encounters in the spirit and at the beginning Jesus explains something about the seven churches in what was at that time called the province of Asia. Revelation 1:12-13, 20 says:

> I turned around to see the voice that was speaking to me. And when I turned I saw seven golden lampstands, and among the lampstands was someone like a son of man, dressed in a robe reaching down to his feet and with a golden sash around his chest. . . . The mystery of the seven stars that you saw in my right hand and of the seven golden lampstands

is this: The seven stars are the angels of the seven churches, and the seven lampstands are the seven churches.

Jesus explains to John that the lampstands (also known as candlesticks or candelabra) don't just represent the seven churches but that they *are* the seven churches (and the phraseology in the Greek supports this). Keep in mind that John is having a spiritual encounter and Jesus is showing him spiritual entities, not physical ones. In that same passage we see that He is also holding seven stars which *are* angels, and we see the terms "angel" and "star" used interchangeably throughout the Old Testament which only further strengthens the point I am making. For some reason, in the spiritual realms each of those seven churches have a spiritual candlestick that represents their entity-hood in the spirit. I suggest this actually applies to all churches and this is significant because it has a few implications.

First, if each church has a lampstand then in order for this to be possible, at some point in the spirit that lampstand must be created. Jesus said exactly zero things about it, and the Apostle Paul said the same—nothing. As there is nothing in all of the Bible or even spiritual traditions of the Church that I am aware of that teaches about lampstand-creation then I can only presume it is something that happens naturally and/or automatically during the process of a church forming and growing. If it wasn't automatic, presumably Jesus would have taught us how to do it. It also means that when we as people gather together and form a local church body that we are contributing together to the formation of a lampstand in the spirit. Second, this means that each church entity has some kind of spiritual existence that can be influenced. Consider that lampstands are designed to hold candles, and candles, whether oil-and-wick, wax, or other mechanism, all emit light and have a flame. In the natural, the color, size, and intensity of a flame are dependent on a series of factors and I would imagine the same is true of the lights that church lampstands emit in the spirit. Regarding the lampstand for the Tabernacle, Exodus 27:20-21 says:

> Command the Israelites to bring you clear oil of pressed olives for the light so that the lamps may be kept burning. In the tent of meeting, outside the curtain that shields the ark of the covenant law, Aaron and his sons are to keep the lamps burning before the Lord from evening till morning. This is to be a lasting ordinance among the Israelites for the generations to come.

Hebrews 9:24 tells us that these natural things such as the temple lampstand are just a *copy* of spiritual things, so if the physical lampstand is a copy of the spiritual lampstand, then there is a need for the spiritual lampstand to continue to be fed with fuel and kept burning as well. This shows us we have a direct impact on the spiritual lampstand itself. Jesus told a parable in Matthew 25 where he spoke about wise and foolish virgins—specifically about those who did and did not have sufficient oil for their lamps to keep burning. If the Old Testament felt it was important enough to create a "lasting ordinance for generations to come" and Jesus both told a parable about this same concept and directly spoke about it in a prophetic appearance in the New Testament, clearly this is an important issue and we would be wise to understand its influence.

Now, if churches all have lampstands, do para-church ministries? After all, they are churchy in nature but don't necessarily have the same focus and yet in many instances they have just as much if not more spiritual engagement and often as many if not more members than many churches. Likewise, if they have lampstands (and I suggest they do) then those presumably will also form around the initiation of the ministry. If we accept that churches and ministries have them, what else has either a lampstand or some other kind of spiritual object or entity-hood that denotes their existence? Is it reasonable to think that cities, states, and nations also have some kind of object in the spirit? After all, they are made up of tons of people and in some cases number in the hundreds of millions. Do that many people gathered together around a common bond influence the existence of a spiritual entity of some kind? I find that highly likely. In fact, non-Christian spiritualists identify the existence of something called "thought-forms" which are essentially the congealed soul energy of people that gather together around certain subjects or issues. Under such auspices, any nation would certainly qualify to have highly developed thought-forms. Considering the Bible points toward this idea and other non-Christian spiritual paths recognize these spiritual entities exist as well, when the available data points to their existence it only seems sensible to me to recognize the truth and then use that information for strategic benefit.

Actually, lampstands aren't the only things we have the ability to create and influence in the spirit. In Chapter 4 we discussed spiritual math and how our prayers get collected in prayer bowls in the heavens before being cast down to the earth as answers. However, has anyone ever thought about where those bowls come from? How big are they? And who decides all of that? The scriptures don't tell us, but there are some things we do know. Each bowl has a defined size, which we know because it is possible to fill them. If something can be filled, then it has a quantity associated with it. If bowls get filled in response to our prayers, and we are the ones who get to decide what we are praying, then *we create new bowls* largely based on our prayers, thoughts, desires, and most of all our faith. This is actually kind of profound. We have the ability to make spiritual containers in response to the things we pray, both individually and corporately. Knowing this, we can intentionally make new ones and intelligently design the parameters for when and how those bowls get filled. Furthermore, this provides a second example (lampstands and now prayer bowls) of where our human choices have the ability to help create spiritual objects. Seeing this in scripture once could be pure chance, but twice suggests this is more than supposition.

If we look at other groups—governments, businesses, community organizations, and any other kind of group I haven't mentioned, does something make them different than a church as far as having a lampstand or other spiritual entity associated with them? I suggest there is no difference. All of them involve people coming together around some kind of common charter, goal, or purpose, and in the same way that having a goal in prayer creates a prayer bowl and forming a church makes a lampstand, purposefully starting any other group is going to form something in the spirit. In fact, on the demonic side the Bible refers to this sort of thing as a "stronghold"—a place where the enemy is able to form a place of spiritual influence due to our involvement in their dark purposes. In spite of that, to keep things simple and clear for this discussion I will refer to everything as having a lampstand.

We are going to look at two well-known charismatic ministries as examples of this in action. Iris Ministries, based in Mozambique, Africa, is headed by Rolland and Heidi Baker. Freedom Ministries, headed by David Hogan, is currently based out of Texas but has had a ministry primarily in Mexico and South America for decades. Both ministries operate very strongly in signs, wonders, and miracles. Both Iris and Freedom Ministries did not begin from day one with a heavy operation in the miraculous, either by their founders or members, but currently they see miracles almost daily somewhere in their ministry and people raised from the dead on a regular basis. Something about their involvement and engagement in things caused them to "level up" in the spirit, and it has been observed over time.

Iris Ministries' first significant level-shift took place after a dramatic series of encounters at the Toronto Airport Christian Fellowship, a church in Toronto, Canada, back in 1994. It was during a series of nightly meetings that lasted for years, an event now known as the Toronto Blessing. God had visited this church in a powerful way, and people were being touched and transformed on a daily, even hourly basis. Heidi and Rolland were burned-out missionaries and this church and these meetings were their last-ditch effort to get help. After their visit and this outpouring from Heaven, during which Heidi had a dramatic series of spiritual encounters, their ministry started to climb to new levels both in the natural and the spiritual. Miracles broke out, but also other things in the physical realm brought expansion and increase in their ministry and from that time forward they have significantly contributed to transformation in Mozambique and surrounding nations.

Freedom Ministries has undergone many transformations as God has visited them deep in the jungles of Mexico and nearby countries. While their leader, David Hogan, has preached on many occasions about some of the visitations they have had from God and other heavenly beings, Freedom Ministries has also dealt with any number of high-level demon spirits controlling various regions of their work, and fighting against black-magic witches and warlocks under demonic control. As they battled through evil spiritual encounters and attacks and overcame, their ministry would hit new levels in the spirit. At times they would see new miracles and breakthroughs as a result.

The point in sharing these examples is to look at a progression toward the miraculous in each ministry that I believe is influenced in part by their lampstand. While in the beginning that lampstand might not have been anything special, something about the prayers and encounters that those ministries have had over time have caused something to shift in the spirit and their lampstands have reached new heights over time. Whether this would look like a bigger lampstand, a stronger or bigger flame, or something else I really couldn't say, but both groups have had a ministry-wide shift over time that impartation and personal spiritual gifts do not account for. For example, if one person flows in a particular miracle then that person will see that miracle occur and others who witness it might have their faith built to experience similar. Through proximity to the person and/or through intentional impartation prayer this would naturally result in a gradual sharing of spiritual gifts to others around that individual, which would be normal to expect. However, when there is a spiritual breakthrough in a ministry and many leaders and congregants who are sometimes separated by physical distance all begin operating in a similarly increased level of supernatural influence, impartation from person to person is not sufficient to explain it. The lampstand serves as a very sensible explanation.

The existence of a spiritual entity means that everyone involved in that organization is tied into it somehow. This doesn't have to be through a formal membership roll necessarily, but through involvement and group-related identification. The lampstand influences the members attached to it and the members attached to it feed into the lampstand, and there is a sort of spiritual symbiosis that occurs. In other words, all group members will likely be included to a greater or lesser degree in the spiritual happenings that influence that lampstand. Breakthroughs in the organization will filter back to the individual based on their connection in the spirit to the lampstand. Likewise, losses, curses, and other problems can be reflected back to the individual as well. Yet, it also seems sensible to recognize that those who are tied into that lampstand more closely will notice more of the benefits and deficits than those who are more loosely connected—although everyone will be affected in some manner.

What is the benefit of knowing that groups have lampstands? It has to do with how each entity functions and grows in the spirit over time, and ties to our ability to make mantles of authority. When we understand that a mantle is related to spiritual authority over something—whether a ministry, government, business, or other organization—then any time a new group is made and a new lampstand is created, a new mantle would also be created at that time. After all, if someone is supposed to be governing or stewarding the lampstand, then the one with the mantle will be the one primarily responsible for it. If there were a finite number of mantles in the earth then business and ministry leaders especially might feel a need to fight over them in hopes of obtaining one for their organization. Yet, because mantles can be shared, divided, and even new ones formed, this isn't an issue at all.

While I suggest that there may be other factors about the subject of mantles that are yet to be fully understood, such as whether one has to either create or be involved in a group in order to make or receive a mantle, I do think we can glean a lot from what the scriptures have already showed us and from things we can observe. The goal isn't to become a mantle-collector, as though more mantles make one more spiritual or more powerful—because that doesn't seem to be the case. Mantles, from what I understand, have more to do with a combination of authority and responsibility. When one has a mantle, they get whatever the benefits of having it are (which remain difficult to quantify), but they also become responsible for the authority they have been given to steward it wisely. James 3:1 says it like this, "Not many of you should become teachers, my fellow believers, because you know that we who teach will be judged more strictly." The goal isn't to have a mantle just to have one, but to get the right mantle for the right job and know or discover when to pass it on to someone else. If a mantle remains with a governing body then when someone leaves that governing body the mantle generally stays behind—and in reality, holding onto it wouldn't benefit the person leaving anyway. To tie this back in to the initial point of when mantles should or shouldn't be passed on, when trying to decide whether to intentionally transfer a mantle or not, it is going to have a lot to do with the relationship that individual has or will have with the purpose behind that specific mantle.

This subject opens up some other questions though. If we accept that each country, church, or business has a lampstand, then what happens when someone's business closes down or a country is taken over? What happens to the lampstand? And what happens with the mantle? Presumably in the case of a company buyout or national takeover, the lampstand and/or mantle of the one either gets absorbed somehow into the other or falls dormant. If a business or ministry closes entirely then either the lampstand and mantle get destroyed, remain dormant in the spirit forever, or lie dormant until someone else picks them up. In some cases it is possible that a group closes down *because* the lampstand or mantle was stolen by the enemy in the spirit. Considering mantles aren't permanent and resident like other spiritual gifts, I think it is generally more beneficial for the individual to engage in their own spiritual growth and receive impartation that endures than it is to try to join some kind of spiritual bidding war for mantles in a process that is, again, very poorly understood, but mantles do have their place. I wish I could explain more about that aspect of the mantle myself but there is still so much we as the Body of Christ don't understand at this time.

The positive side of this issue of lost, stolen, broken, and abandoned mantles is that many of them may be available to us now.

Many prophets, especially in the Charismatic Movement over the past few decades, have prophesied that God is revealing and re-releasing old mantles to the Body. Most commonly people refer to big-name ministers such as John G Lake, Smith Wigglesworth, William Branham, Kathryn Kuhlman, and even Apostles and Old Testament prophets when prophesying about old mantles that are going to be used once again, but there are far more than just those available to the Body of Christ to be redeemed in this hour. And while that is exciting on the one hand, a reminder, again, is that we need the right mantle for the right job, and having one doesn't benefit us if we don't have an outlet to utilize it properly.

Whether we are talking about some aspect of mantles, lampstands, or spiritual entities, all of these can be strategically utilized to assist our spiritual advancement. The goal of mantles is to use those that we do receive in the most effective manner possible, and the same applies for lampstands, prayer bowls, and all other tools God has created for us. As we learn and grow in these areas we will find that, like impartation, they can be strategically implemented in ways that accelerate us far beyond what we expect.

Chapter 10

Wisdom for Laying on of Hands

The primary method used to impart virtue from one person to another is laying on of hands. For those not familiar with the term, it literally means to place your hands on someone else's body (usually on a hand, shoulder, back, or sometimes the top of the head) and pray for that individual to receive the power of the Holy Spirit. The Bible has verses that encourage this practice but others that provide a warning, so we are going to discuss some things people need to understand about what happens when we lay hands on one another to help us do it wisely.

As we have already covered, impartation is a term describing the release of spiritual virtue from one person to another. In 2 Timothy 1:6 Paul wrote to his disciple Timothy and stated, "For this reason I remind you to fan into flame the gift of God, which is in you through the laying on of my hands." In this passage, Paul described a particular spiritual gift that he gave to Timothy through the process of laying hands on him. It is assumed from the context that Timothy was aware of what this gift was although Paul did not explicitly state it in the text. When Paul put his hands on Timothy's body and prayed for him, Paul transferred spiritual substance from his life to Timothy's. A good comparison is that of a magnetic card reader commonly used in stores that transfer funds from a debit card to a merchant's account. When the card connects with the reader, a nontangible transaction takes place, but even though the transaction itself is invisible and takes place in hyperspace, funds are still transferred. Impartation works in the same way, but this is only one of the reasons for laying on of hands.

Another use for this practice is to commission people into positions of authority. Acts 6:1-6 shows us an example of this with the apostles laying hands on seven men and commissioning them to manage the needs of the widows so the apostles could spend more time on other aspects of ministry. The men were first chosen, and when the apostles officially installed them into their new positions they all had a time of prayer, laying hands on the new leaders. If one were to intentionally transfer a mantle, as discussed in the previous chapter, laying on of hands would be one way to do this.

Healing the sick is yet another reason why we might lay hands on someone. Mark 16:17-18 says, "And these signs will accompany those who believe: In my name . . . they will place their hands on sick people, and they will get well." Praying to heal the sick can be done in several ways, but there is something about placing our hands on someone that can help transfer the power of God, imparting healing to their body. James 5:14 says, "Is anyone among you sick? Let them call the elders of the church to pray over them and anoint them with oil in the name of the Lord." The process of anointing someone with oil typically involves rubbing or smearing it on them, which could be interpreted as a form of laying on of hands as well. Regardless of the exact details, this practice is well-known in relation to healing the sick.

Given that there are multiple reasons one can lay hands on others, Paul writes something slightly confusing (and if we are honest, somewhat disconcerting) to Timothy as well. In 1 Timothy 5:22 Paul expresses a warning about laying hands on people, saying "Do not be hasty in the laying on of hands, and do not share in the sins of others. Keep yourself pure." There is a bit of debate in Christian circles as to the exact meaning of this verse but when we consider that commissioning people into leadership roles is one of the possibilities and 1 Timothy 5 talks mostly about instructions for leading, it seems sensible that this could be what the passage was talking about. However, it doesn't actually specify and there are other factors that leave it open to a broader interpretation. From a wisdom perspective Paul's warning to Timothy has a number of implications, which we will discuss.

THE DARK SIDE OF IMPARTATION

If we think about Paul's warning of "sharing sins," this suggests that something about the mechanism of impartation means there is the potential to share negative attributes as well as positive ones. While it would be nice if impartation only ever applied to good things, it is a universal spiritual principle. What this means is that anyone can do it, including those who serve powers of darkness. In fact, some dark occult groups have older members intentionally transfer their powers to younger members just before they die to encourage continued growth and strengthening of their ranks through the years.

Someone doesn't have to be in the occult for this type of negative-transfer to occur either. Many years ago, when I was in a ministry training school, I was up near the front of the sanctuary praying for people at the end of a church service during the "altar call" time. I was paired up with another student, Julia, and a man approached the two of us asking for prayer. I don't recall what the prayer was for, but when he approached, I had the distinct impression in my spirit that under no circumstances was he to touch Julia, or her him. However, it would have been both extremely awkward to say that aloud at the time and probably somewhat hurtful to him as well, as I had no idea why I was sensing that so strongly from the Holy Spirit. I made sure to subtly position myself to add a layer of physical disconnect between her and him but still have the man get the prayer ministry he needed. I simply had him and I hold hands while we prayed and Julia put her hand on my shoulder, thus no direct contact between the two. After we finished praying and the man left, Julia confirmed to me that she had the same leading I did about the physical contact as well. Keep in mind that nothing in this story is meant to suggest that man was evil or doing something wrong—just that something about laying on of hands was going to cause a problem for one or both of them. There are several reasons we could have gotten that strong leading, which we will examine.

Now, some would argue that in order to avoid the above situation that men should only ever minister to men and women should only ever pray for women, and that stems largely but not exclusively from concerns about sexual impropriety. I personally reject that notion. While certainly there are times and situations where we need to use wisdom with the opposite gender, anyone who has issues with homosexuality isn't going to be better-served with rigid gender-based prayer rules, and it entirely ignores what the Holy Spirit may want to do in that moment. If a female operates in a certain spiritual gift that a man needs, then that's what he needs, and Heaven isn't going to withhold it because we think she is the wrong gender to minister to him, or vice versa. Furthermore, in our situation we weren't ministering privately and were standing in a sanctuary in full view of hundreds of people so nothing sexually inappropriate was going to occur anyway. The men-with-men and women-with-women thing is a deeply entrenched, harmful religious mindset that rarely reflects the heart of God for situations and has more to do with placating the fears of mankind than it has to do with wisdom in leadership. If we were talking about concerns with a *private* meeting, the only reasonable claim is that meeting with any individual of *either* gender alone could be a problem, because it isn't a gender-specific issue and to believe it is seems nearsighted and lacking in discernment.

The primary underlying issue with prayer ministry of any kind, at least as it relates to impartation, is that of transference—and while that is the point of impartation, it is important to take steps to ensure that only positive attributes move from one person to another. Any number of things can happen when we lay hands on someone. Certainly they can receive healing or other spiritual virtue, but demons also like to jump from person to person the same way. Back in my college years some friends came over to our apartment and my roommates and I were hanging out with them. One of the guys complained about a headache he had—which started just after he laid hands on his brother and prayed for his brother's headache to go away roughly an hour prior. His brother's pain went away but then his started. This is a classic example of a demon transferring from one person to another. Instead of addressing the headache, we took authority over the evil spirit causing it, cast it out, and the pain instantly left. This is one more reason we must be discerning when we lay hands on others. In fact, it's possible this is the reason why Julia and I felt such a strong leading when praying for that other man. That, or there could have been some other spiritual baggage that would have been shared which could have been equally unhealthy. If we recall how in an earlier chapter we looked at how we pass on some of the "flavor" of our own human spirit during the impartation process, sometimes we can also share some aspect of our inner issues and not just the good stuff. And for those who have ever walked away from praying with someone feeling like they got "slimed," that is probably what happened.

When we lay hands on someone, we end up connecting with their soul and spirit. Something about the physical contact with their body facilitates that connection, and something about that contact engenders a form of attraction or favor between the two parties. In healthy relationships this can actually be a good thing, helping draw members in the Body of Christ closer to one another. In unhealthy relationships this has the potential to foment hidden attractions and hinder healthy relationships. Again, this isn't a gender-specific issue and shouldn't be treated as one—it is important to understand and be discerning any time we lay hands on someone.

THE SHIELD OF FAITH

While discernment is very important, there are things we can do in our own lives and hearts that help reduce or mitigate any negative influences that seek to attach themselves during times of prayer and impartation. The benefit of mitigating these issues is that it reduces fear—we don't need to feel like bad things are out to get us when someone just wants to bless us in prayer. In fact, if the takeaway from this chapter is that impartation has more risks than benefits then things have been badly miscommunicated. We do need to be wise, but our approach to impartation can help us walk in freedom in this area. There is a key hidden in Ephesians 6, the section about the armor of God, which is of immense use. While it may sound incredibly cliché to say "just use the armor of God," I have never heard this particular detail taught in the way I'm going to explain it, so I feel it is important to share. Ephesians 6:16 says, "In addition to all this, take up the shield of faith, with which you can extinguish all the flaming arrows of the evil one." While yes, it should seem obvious that shields would be protective, the issue isn't that a shield protects. The issue is *what* the shield is made of. Normally we think of faith as accomplishing something, but this passage tells us that *faith is protective.* Why would the apostle Paul tell us to use our faith as a shield to protect us from enemy attacks? Because it can and does.

110

I'm not just talking about general life issues that we have to deal with and we can say "my faith in God helps me through this" although it will do that. I'm talking about faith that is actively and intentionally applied toward the purpose of self-protection.

I want to use an extreme example found in scripture, and then we will look at this in context of impartation. Isaiah 43:2 tells us:

> When you pass through the waters, I will be with you; and when you pass through the rivers, they will not sweep over you. When you walk through the fire, you will not be burned; the flames will not set you ablaze.

This is a cool-sounding verse that if we take on a highly interpretive level it says "God will protect me always." If we take it at face value, however, this verse tells us that we can fearlessly walk even through forest fires and massive flooding with no concern for our lives because it doesn't matter which kind of natural disaster we are dealing with—we will be perfectly safe.

But what about all of those believers who have died in house fires or drowned in oceans, rivers, or lakes? Where was this fire-and-water protection for them? I don't know—and discussing this isn't me questioning their faith. What I do know is that when we intentionally activate our faith related to these verses and *expect* that we are safe in fire or water, we will get better results than if we don't. In other words, a shield is usually only effective when we actually use it. If we have a shield hanging on our arm but never protect our body with it, we have a heavy arm-decoration and not a shield. Sure, we might get lucky on occasion and the shield blocks something, but that's simply a matter of probabilities—if something comes in the right direction and the shield happens to be in the way, it gets blocked. However, if we activate our faith and are intentional about where we apply it, we will find that enemy attacks are far less effective because we place the shield in line with the spiritual attack. When I talk about "applying faith" I am referring to specifically developing beliefs that align with our ever-protectedness in Christ and praying regularly to live in a state of safety. Intentionally doing these things activates our faith and uses it to shield us from the powers of darkness arrayed against us.

How does this apply to impartation? Luke 11:13 says, "If you then, though you are evil, know how to give good gifts to your children, how much more will your Father in heaven give the Holy Spirit to those who ask him!" Personally, I don't believe in receiving darkness through prayer. I recognize it can happen, but I don't believe in it happening to *me*. Any time I receive prayer my expectation is that because I'm asking for good things, I will *only* receive things that are from God—the Radiant Being of Love and Light who only gives good and perfect gifts. Titus 1:15a says, "To the pure, all things are pure." If we want to receive things that are pure and good, then we exert our faith up-front to say, "Only good things are allowed to come to me, and I am shielded against receiving bad things because I believe that if I ask for good, that is all I will get!" Because I use my faith as a protection against receiving evil, that's typically what happens. Still, we also must follow the leading of the Holy Spirit and regardless of what we extend our faith toward. If He warns us to not touch someone, not pray certain things, or any other kind of warning then we need to heed those instructions.

THE EYE GATE

We are going to look at another way we can impart to others that isn't through the laying on of hands—impartation through the eyes, eye contact, or eyesight. It is important we understand this to truly round out our knowledge on the subject, and we are going to begin with some scriptures and then examples of how this can work for both good and evil. We could have discussed this early on when looking at how impartation works, but it seemed to be a better fit for this chapter.

The Bible mentions the word "eye" 564 times. In the vast number of cases, it is referring to something that an individual physically witnessed or is using the term as part of flowery, metaphoric language (ex. finding favor in your eyes; doing evil in the eyes of the Lord). However, there are a few passages that aren't referring to physical eyes and the expressions sound both potentially metaphorical but also referencing mysteries—hidden truths of the spiritual realm. For example, the Bible speaks in multiple places of opening people's eyes to see spiritual things: in Numbers 22:31 with Balaam and an angel, 2 Kings 6:17 with Elisha and a servant surrounded by enemy armies, and in Ephesians 1:18 where Paul mentions the "eyes of the heart." There is a definite connection between these spiritual eyes and light.

We see this connection in multiple places in scripture. Psalm 13:3 says, "Look on me and answer, Lord my God. Give light to my eyes, or I will sleep in death. . ." If David did not receive light into his eyes, he would die. Now, presumably this is talking about spiritual light and not physical, but even that is something found throughout scripture beginning in Genesis 1. In Genesis 1:1-4 it is the first day of creation and God creates light. Yet, in verse 14 it is the fourth day of creation when He creates the sun and moon to hang in the sky and give light to the world. Now, if God made light four creation-days before the objects that we know produce physical light, then the first light he created was spiritual in nature and not temporal. The Bible makes further connections between light and life in the person of Jesus, saying in John 1:1-5:

In the beginning was the Word, and the Word was with God, and the Word was God. He was with God in the beginning. Through him all things were made; without him nothing was made that has been made. In him was life, and that life was the light of all mankind. The light shines in the darkness, and the darkness has not overcome it.

When we understand the close connection between life, spiritual light, and our own human spirits and spiritual eyes, then certain verses make a little more sense. We see in 1 Samuel 14:27 that Jonathan eats some honey and it brings light to his eyes, but why would honey do that? Well, normally it wouldn't but they hadn't eaten for days and when he ate food it brought life and vitality to his body and presumably helped enliven his spirit, as evidenced through the light coming into his eyes. We see the converse of this in Job 17:7 which states, "My eyes have grown dim with grief; my whole frame is but a shadow." Where life brightens the eyes, death and sorrow make one's spirit, and thus one's eyes, grow dim. And yet, we see that obedience to God can also bring spiritual light back. Psalm 19:8b tells us, "The commands of the Lord are radiant, giving light to the eyes."

With this connection between light, life, and spiritual eyes in mind, Jesus says some things in the gospel of Matthew (also in Luke 11:34) that are of particular interest. In Matthew 6:22-23 He says, "The eye is the lamp of the body. If your eyes are healthy, your whole body will be full of light. But if your eyes are unhealthy, your whole body will be full of darkness. If then the light within you is darkness, how great is that darkness!" The eyes are the lamp of the body, which I suggest indicates that they are the means by which the rest of the body receives light. However, there is a crossover connection here between physical and spiritual eyes and physical and spiritual light.

In other words, while the physical organs including the eyes and optic nerves are used to identify physical light and convert it into images, there is something about the organs of our physical body that connect with our spiritual capacity to engage spiritual light. Thus, if our spiritual eyes are healthy then our entire being in spirit, soul, and body will be filled with holy light. There is one more thing about eyes being likened to a lamp and that is that a lamp *emits* light—and this has implications related to impartation.

When we understand that revelation in the spirit is typically released as light from heaven that enters our spiritual eyes and brings information and transformation, then this connection between the eyes and impartation becomes more apparent. Ephesians 1:18 points to this saying, "I pray that the eyes of your heart may be enlightened in order that you may know the hope to which he has called you, the riches of his glorious inheritance in his holy people. . ." and this is because the spiritual eyes receive the light of revelation. We have already covered in a previous chapter how revelation from heaven can function as a form of impartation, but if the eyes are the lamp of the body and emit light, does that mean we can directly pass spiritual light from one person to another through our eyes? It does.

One of the things I have learned over the years is that there is far more that is possible to do in the spirit than we have any concept, and one of those hidden abilities is the capacity to transmit through the eyes. In fact, witches tend to make use of this ability intentionally, especially when out in public. They do what I call "demonic layering" which is where when making eye contact with someone they intentionally add curses onto a person who has been marked by the enemy in the spirit. This happens most often with victims of Satanic Ritual Abuse (SRA) but it can happen to anyone. In the spirit the servant of darkness can see some measure of the demonic structures and markings that have been attached to that person, and their goal is to casually strengthen whatever their people, our enemy, are doing.

When out in public, we will all from time to time make random eye contact with a person—whether in a store or driving down the road. In some cases, we make that eye contact and move on, but those times where we and he or she hold that contact for seconds on end, what is happening there? Has anyone ever wondered what it is about that individual that causes us to continue staring into each other's eyes even though we don't know each other at all and may never see one another again our entire lives? In those instances, something is happening in the spirit and we are connecting with them through our eye contact. Now, it requires discernment to realize whether we are making a bad connection, where the demonic in him/her and the demonic beings not-yet-expelled from us are passing curses, energy, and other resources back and forth, or whether the Holy Spirit and our human spirits are doing something intentional and good with that person. In the case of the former, it is important to pray and break off any demonic connections and reject anything that was imparted in that moment, as well as ask the Lord to reveal what access the enemy has in our lives so we can remove it permanently. In the case of the latter, we can pray to bless that person and whatever God is doing in and through them. Yet, either or both are possible and we need to be aware that sometimes eye contact isn't as simple as it appears.

While it is true that the enemy uses this ability, we can use it too. We are going to look at a story a friend of mine, Colleen, shared with me once that shows us how we can use this ability to bring life to those around us. We will end the chapter here on a high note, and then in the following chapter will look at how we can use the many things we have covered in this book to develop a culture of spiritual power. Her testimony is as follows:

Even though I am retired now, I worked with young children for 25 years—4 and 5 year olds at this particular time. This particular year we had a lot of ADHD children and kids with other diagnosed disorders. It was a very hectic class!

After learning through Arthur Burk's materials about calling someone's spirit forward and blessing that spirit, I openly used it in the classroom. I would let children know that if they felt bad, in any way, that I would be happy to "Give them some 'eye to eye' time." That is what I called it so that the school and parents would not get a sense about what I was actually doing.

Children would come to me and I would tell them to look into my eyes and past my eyes and find 'the heart of love that I have for them' and I told them that I would do the same to 'find their heart of love for me.' I would know when we were connected through a shift in their expression. It's like a quiet joyful peace took over their face as I opened my heart to theirs. Their whole countenance would relax.

At that moment I would start blessing them with whatever Holy Spirit told me that they needed, like peace, joy, confidence etc. I would bless them 'in the name of the one who loves them more than any person could', in the name of 'the author of love' etc. I'd instruct their spirit to connect with that Person of Love.

I had one particular sweet boy that was high-functioning autistic. He would spend a lot of time tracing the room with his finger and tracing the activities with his finger. I asked him one particular day if he would like some 'eye to eye time' and he came over to me. That was an amazing thing in itself.

But he had seen me do this with others many times, and I had taken special care to show this little guy love! He stood a little farther away from me, but as we looked into each other's eyes, looking past the surface, he inched closer. When our spirits connected and I started blessing him, pouring into his spirit, he leaned his head towards me and let his forehead rest on my forehead. Understand that he never liked to be touched! As our heads touched, a smile came on his face as he looked deep into my eyes. He stayed connected with me for a long time, and I just kept on pouring the love in! It was the sweetest moment!

That was just an example, but my co teachers would sometimes comment on how much calmer the kids were after their eye to eye time! Truly remarkable!

-Colleen-

Chapter 11

The Importance of Stewardship

In this book we have focused intensely on the subject of impartation for the purpose of growing in spiritual power, and for good reason—power is necessary to destroy works of darkness and to display the works of God in the earth. Even Jesus needed it. Acts 10:38 tells us, ". . . how God anointed Jesus of Nazareth with the Holy Spirit and power, and how he went around doing good and healing all who were under the power of the devil, because God was with him." Spiritual power is a vital part of our Christian walk, and one that often gets pushed aside in favor of other things. And yet, despite its usefulness, there are issues that more power simply won't solve. Furthermore, there are always those who object to the need to operate in increasing levels of spiritual power in favor of growing in the fruit of the Spirit. The truth is that if we want to properly steward anything spiritual, especially the power of God, we *must* grow in character.

If we read Galatians, we see that Paul is writing to a church that is having issues with settling back into legalism after being set free from the law through the gospel of Jesus Christ. He speaks to that church about walking in the Spirit instead of under law, but then he addresses their behaviors and emotions. Galatians 5:16-23 (with verse references left in for reference) says:

16 So I say, walk by the Spirit, and you will not gratify the desires of the flesh. 17 For the flesh desires what is contrary to the Spirit, and the Spirit what is contrary to the flesh. They are in conflict with each other, so that you are not to do whatever you want. 18 But if you are led by the Spirit, you are not under the law.

19 The acts of the flesh are obvious: sexual immorality, impurity and debauchery; 20 idolatry and witchcraft; hatred, discord, jealousy, fits of rage, selfish ambition, dissensions, factions 21 and envy; drunkenness, orgies, and the like. I warn you, as I did before, that those who live like this will not inherit the kingdom of God.

22 But the fruit of the Spirit is love, joy, peace, forbearance, kindness, goodness, faithfulness, 23 gentleness and self-control. Against such things there is no law.

The initial point in this passage (v16-18) is that we are to live in concert with the Holy Spirit and not the desires of our sinful nature and/or "flesh," but then Paul goes on to elaborate in v19 on what the works of the flesh and the fruit of the Spirit are. It is important to note that the works of the flesh (v19) are a combination of actions or behaviors and negative emotions, while the fruit of the Spirit (v22) appear to be largely based on healthy emotion and/or a healthy soul—all of which *comes* from the Spirit. This is an important distinction to note because unhealthy behaviors are largely the result of unhealthy emotions and beliefs. As we are talking about the fruit of the Spirit in relation to growing in spiritual power, we need to understand that if we want to steward the power of God effectively, it will require us to grow in character as well.

There are some who believe we must either prioritize character over power or perform some sort of ongoing balancing act between the two, as if we are comparing stacks of paper and adding a little bit to whichever stack is shorter at the time. It doesn't work like that. If we want to prioritize character, the *fruit* of the Spirit, over the *gifts* of the same Spirit then we are ignoring the fact that they both come from *the same Spirit.* The fact is that we need both, and we need both in ever-increasing quantities. The thing about character is that it generally can't be imparted the same way we can release spiritual power one to another. If you think about it, it's in the names—gifts are given but fruit is grown. Impartation can instantly take us into new levels of power, but fruit doesn't generally work like that. Can you imagine how nice it would be if it did though? We wouldn't have to discover all the ways in which we are selfish or unloving as revealed through our relationships with one another—our spouses, kids, coworkers, and friends. None of that Hebrews 5:8 "Although He was a Son, He learned obedience from the things which He suffered." (NASB) nonsense. We could simply have someone lay hands on us and BOOM! Insta-Saint!

First Corinthians explains a bit about why character is so necessary and how walking in power, while incredibly important, isn't the pinnacle of spirituality. 1 Corinthians 13:1-3 says:

> If I speak in the tongues of men or of angels, but do not have love, I am only a resounding gong or a clanging cymbal. If I have the gift of prophecy and can fathom all mysteries and all knowledge, and if I have a faith that can move mountains, but do not have love, I am nothing. If I give all I possess to the poor and give over my body to hardship that I may boast, but do not have love, I gain nothing.

The Power of Impartation

This short passage has tons of information in it, but if we boil it all down, it basically says that love is the goal. Jesus told us in John 15:13 that the greatest act of love is that of sacrificing our lives for a friend. It doesn't matter how many spiritual gifts we operate in or how big our faith is, love absolutely *must* be the foundation. And yet, that doesn't in any way diminish the significant importance of spiritual power either. After all, Paul was the one who also said, "I thank God that I speak in tongues more than all of you. . ." (1 Corinthians 14:18) and also, "Follow the way of love and eagerly desire gifts of the Spirit, especially prophecy." (1 Corinthians 14:1). Sometimes people read 1 Corinthians 13 as though it is anti-gifts or that power is less important than character. Paul doesn't actually ever say that, and neither should we. In fact, if we truly look at how he speaks of them, they are inseparable—or at least they should be.

The pitfall in growing in spiritual power while lacking in character is that we will become prideful, often belittling others and/or valuing them less because we perceive ourselves as having something they don't. And it's not always possible to perfectly avoid either. Knowing we must grow in the fruit of the Spirit doesn't mean that we will always do it successfully either. It just means that the Holy Spirit will continue to lead and guide us into all truth, often in spite of ourselves.

Let me give you an example in my own life of what this can look like when done completely wrong. Over a decade and a half ago, when I first began learning how to operate in spiritual gifts, I was in college and had two roommates. The church I went to was Charismatic, in that they believed in and practiced spiritual gifts, but I was eager to experience everything that was possible as far as those things were concerned. My friend and mentor Diane would often get what is known as being "drunk in the Spirit" when the Holy Spirit came upon her during church services, and I wanted to have that experience too. Because I was so hungry for God-encounters, a few times I went to meetings held by other campus groups where cool spiritual stuff was happening. One of those meetings was hosted by a church called Antioch where my friend Jen went. She told me about a guest speaker they had invited, a preacher named Paul Cox, and I was excited to attend because I had already heard of him and what God was doing in his ministry. At the meeting that night God touched me powerfully and after that I began to have this kind of twitch-shake-thing that would happen from time to time. This was the beginning of my experiences with spiritual manifestations such as being drunk in the spirit, but what happened was that I got so focused on those experiences that I started to develop a mental hierarchy in my mind that basically valued people who were having those encounters over those who weren't. Looking back on that I can see how utterly ridiculous that was, but at the time it didn't seem that way. I was spiritually immature and very new to all of this so was bound to make mistakes, and I certainly did so.

I remember two distinct times when someone had to verbally put me in my place, and in both instances, they were entirely right to do so. Once was with my friend Ashod who was training to be a campus minister at the time, as was I. We were over at his apartment one evening and I said something about replacing the current campus pastors because we were clearly more eager than they were and they seemed to have lost their zeal. He immediately told me how incredibly prideful that was—and he was right. I had ignored their extensive experience and ongoing sacrifices they made to be campus ministers and decided that they weren't "on fire" enough when in fact what was largely the case was they had a lot of wisdom I lacked and some of the decisions they made that I disagreed with were based not out of laziness or lack of engagement but out of a wealth of past experience and them discerning what the Holy Spirit was and was not doing. The other time was during the manifestation-obsession phase. The Holy Spirit spoke to Diane during one of her prayer times and she told me something I will probably never forget. She said, "You have become enamored with manifestations." "Enamored" is not a word that gets used much, and it struck to the heart of the issue. The moment she said that, I realized that I had gotten very far off course with things and it upset me—not because she hurt my feelings, but because I realized just how badly I was messing up and it has always been my heart to walk out this faith journey well. I apologized to her, my roommates, and others as well, but those were moments where my need for character growth poked through in the middle of my pursuit of spiritual power.

We are all going to make mistakes on this journey, and we will all need friends to tell us just how badly we are missing it from time to time. Proverbs 27:5 tells us, "Better is open rebuke than hidden love." If we cultivate healthy, transparent friendships then when we need those open rebukes we will get them—and our friends will love us just as much if not more afterward for how we receive their loving concern and addressing the issues. It is important that we don't stop moving forward and growing in the power of the Spirit just because we have character issues, but it is vital that we are just as intentional about character growth as we are about impartation and related matters. I am personally a huge proponent of emotional healing because it is a highly effective way that we can rid ourselves of the root issues that stir up negative emotions and cause unhealthy behaviors. In fact, when we see ministers who get exposed publicly for any kind of sin issue, I believe it is far more indicative of emotional brokenness that the enemy used to create problems than anything else because I believe that no one is inherently a bad person. Yet, as we grow in the spirit and we find ourselves stepping into new levels of power and authority, we will find that the stakes are bigger and the enemy will often start throwing more temptation and bigger problems at us to slow us down. The more visible we are in any position of spiritual influence, the wiser we must be with our words and actions, and the more we need to receive inner healing and be intentional about character growth so we can properly steward the power God has given us.

Chapter 12

Building a Culture of Power

Imagine a church or other ministry where the focus isn't on training children how to sit and listen to a sermon or to know when to sit and stand at the right places in church ceremonies. What if Sunday school involved teaching Bible stories about healing the sick and then finding sick or injured people present and healing them? What about instead of telling a story about manna appearing to Moses and the Israelites and then handing out crackers, that everyone present listened to the story and then prayed together to watch manna appear on the table in front of them? And what if this wasn't just talking about teaching kids? What if we could actually teach and train adults to not just hear about the power of God but to perform the kinds of signs, wonders, and miracles we see all throughout the Bible?

Tons of people have already left and many more continue to leave what is known as the "institutional church" these days. I did it years ago and haven't looked back. Does that mean I am "anti-church?" Not at all. I have close friends who are pastors and I am supportive of the work they do. Does that mean I no longer gather with other believers? Of course not. And does it mean I would never go to a more traditional church again? No. It just means that I, like many others, don't find the same value in church-as-it-has-always-been-done-before. Why is that? For many, it has to do with the power of God. Why can some believers go to church their entire lives and yet never recall a time they saw God do a miracle? Or almost as bad, that they have only seen God supernaturally intervene in their lives once or twice, seemingly at His random Divine whim? How do we expect to disciple nations full of people without the wonder-working power of God regularly active in our lives? It should be easy for any follower of Jesus to recall scores of times they have seen God's power at work through healings, miracles, signs, and wonders and not years of hoping and wondering if God actually even cares enough about us to intervene.

Isaiah 9:7a says prophetically of Jesus that, "Of the increase of his government and peace there will be no end . . ." The message is straightforward. Jesus doesn't plan to let the enemy govern the world with mayhem and destruction—so much so that His government in this world will *only* continue to increase and never decrease. While this is a view that is counter to many end-times beliefs, Jesus trained his initial followers to make disciples of all nations precisely *because* the goal was to advance and never remain or retrogress. I suggest that the power of impartation is actually a key God has given us to do exactly this—and not just with a few of us, but with all of us!

For decades we have been taught in Church History of the spiritual "greats"—men and women who accessed a higher level of spiritual power or authority or faith or anointing or something else in Christ, but whatever it was, they saw more of the power of God displayed in their lives by far than anyone around them. We hear of people like John G. Lake, William Branham, Kathryn Kuhlman, and Smith Wigglesworth who operated in high levels of healings and miracles. If we read back a bit further in church history, we find men and women like Vincent Ferrere, Joseph of Cupertino, Catherine of Siena, Anthony of Padua, Brigid of Kildare, and Padre Pio. In fact, we can find hundreds of men and women throughout recorded history who have operated in the miraculous who we can list alongside Biblical figures such as Jesus, Moses, Elijah, Elisha, Peter, Stephen, and Paul. And yet, if the Body of Christ around the world numbers in the billions throughout history up to the present, how is it that we haven't grasped these things at such a level that they have become normal, even daily for most followers of Jesus? We are in a period of time where we are seeing the shift from elevated superstar-individual ministry to a group-focus where everyone is "doing the stuff" and ministering with the power of God. I had a dream once that illustrates this shift:

> I was greeting people at a combination wedding-and-coronation. One of the people I greeted was the main character from the movie *Superstar* which was released in 1999. I never referred to her by her name but called her "Superstar" during the entire dream. Two very short girls in their twenties were also present, both wearing high heels. As they removed their heels, they became roughly the height of someone with dwarfism, but of the type with normal body proportions. One girl dropped into the background of the dream, but the other one remained in the foreground and I became aware that she had back pain associated with an injury.
>
> I turned back to Superstar, who was suddenly morbidly obese—all of that weight was put on in-between the time I greeted her and then was with the "little people." Superstar had the same type of injury and back pain. Both she and the little woman needed prayer for healing, but I only prayed for the short woman. As I prayed, she fell over slain in the spirit, and her back was instantly healed. In the dream I knew that God was touching her and not Superstar at that time, so I didn't even try to pray for Superstar. Then the dream ended.

This dream makes a comparison within the body of Christ between those who are seen as "Superstars" and everyone else—the "Little People." In this dream, the term "little people" isn't derogatory—it is a play on words using interpretive language to demonstrate a concept. In the dream, the Little People really are quite physically small, but they try to make themselves appear bigger than they are—all because they're trying to "measure up" to the Superstar. However, when they stop trying to measure up and in humility step down from their posturing, choosing to be themselves over a fabricated image they were projecting, they step into the blessings from heaven that God is releasing. The Superstar has become obese which is suggestive of both a level of spiritual laziness as well as a poor internal state setting up the conditions for the obesity. She isn't just obese, but morbidly obese, which suggests that the Superstars are a "dying breed" so to speak. Unlike in the movie, Superstar is older in the dream whereas the Little People are in their twenties, at a normal "fertile" age to reproduce.

What God is saying in this dream is that the day of the superstars is coming to a close as the old breed dies out in favor of the new. Prophetically, the movie itself aired in 1999, the last year of a millennium, the end of an era. The once-unknown "Little People" are being positioned to stop emulating popular opinion of the spiritual order of the day and instead to uniquely receive and manifest God's grace as they humble themselves and get real with those around them. It is the time where they are being linked even more deeply with Christ and are rising into authority as mature sons and daughters of God and raising up disciples just like them.

This Little People theme is important to understand but needs some clarification. The above dream is referring not just to people of little power or of minimal spiritual influence, but speaks to the removal or at least reduction of celebrity status in Christianity. Many spiritually powerful people are hidden and/or unknown by human standards, yet while their names may never be listed as keynote conference speakers, these giants of faith are taking the spirit realm by storm. And in truth, it is necessary for this to occur. After all, an analogy of little people only travels so far. As we grow in the spirit, we should *all* be growing more spiritually powerful and seeing the virtue of God displayed in greater measure in our lives. As we each reach a place of greater spiritual maturity, we will be great examples to those around us. Instead of having precious few superstars to look up to, the Body of Christ will be full of strong examples of godly living, where each of us can say as Paul did in 1 Corinthians 11:1, "Follow my example, as I follow the example of Christ." After all, the original purpose of superstars was only to show everyone else what is possible to attain to, not for us to perpetually elevate them above all others.

This dream and this message is in part about building a culture of power in the Body of Christ. One of the key benefits of impartation is that we can work together to build this culture among ourselves without having to wait for some big-named person to come visit us and pray for us. In certain kinds of video games there is something called "power-leveling" where a lower-level player joins up with a higher-level player, and while the low-level player adds very little to the party at first, the goal is to get him or her to advance far faster than would have been possible on their own. Related to Christianity and impartation, the idea is that those who are mature in the faith and operate in a greater level of spiritual power can help newer believers to rapidly advance in all things Kingdom. This requires a measure of personal sacrifice up-front, modeling our behavior, authority, wisdom, and experience to those we disciple. By doing this, our disciples will advance spiritually far beyond their own

131

capabilities in a shorter period of time, and the Kingdom as a whole advances. We will find that as we propel others forward that we share in the experiences and revelation they gain and the time and energy we spend with others will usually help us in the long run as well.

I mentioned before that many people are leaving the traditional or institutional church in search of the power of God—and in many cases, in search of the person of God Himself. One doesn't *have* to leave the church they are in if they want to see God's power flow through their life (though some may feel led to); it is possible to do this whether in a traditional church or outside of one. In fact, the only prerequisite is that we be His followers and it has nothing to do with whether/where we do or do not attend church. However, if we want to advance rapidly then positioning matters—which is why we need to develop a spiritual culture where we don't just hope things are going to happen, but where we take an active role in changing them.

In the past few decades there have been ministry schools appearing all over the world whose basic purpose is to train believers for supernatural ministry, essentially creating power-leveling training for everyone who attends. The benefit of these kinds of schools is that they tend to focus on prophetic gifts, divine healing, and the miraculous—all of which help the believer to learn and hone their skills in these areas. Typically, there is also a measure of impartation that occurs throughout the training that helps advance the students even further. All of these things are good for the believer to learn, and many of these schools have a lot of fruit of teaching people to flow in supernatural ministry to heal the sick, prophesy hope into bad situations, and ultimately manifest the power of God in problem situations. But what if it were time to take things to another level?

While it is good that we have ministry training schools for this sort of thing, what would happen if entire churches caught the vision of acceleration through impartation? What would happen if people got so hungry for signs, wonders, and miracles that they became incredibly intentional about imparting to one another regularly, and in some cases daily?

Building a culture of power is going to look different depending on where we go, as each group will have their own dynamics, but at its core I suggest this type of Kingdom culture values demonstrating the love of God *through* the power of God. We see in John 3:16 that Jesus came to the earth because God loves us. And yet, when Jesus came what we saw Him teach can largely be summed up into two key words: *Love* and *Power*. He was explicitly clear in John 13:35 that love is what sets us apart and shows others we are His disciples, yet he also told his closest disciples in John 14:11, only 14 verses later in that same monologue, that if people can't believe in Him then they need to look on the evidence of miracles He displayed for them.

I personally have been very intentional about this throughout my life. The reason I began to encounter the heavenly gems I write about in my book *Gemstones From Heaven* is because after being introduced to a minister and his wife who operate regularly in that miracle, I invited them to come to our home for a series of meetings. I knew that if they came, the miracles would too, and I very intentionally invited people in order to have them encounter miracles. By the same token, I am fairly picky about the kinds of conferences and events I attend. I discovered years ago that any kind of event or gathering has its own flavor or energy about it, whether in the church or not, and this has helped me to choose what kind of energy I want flowing in my life. If I want to succeed at sales and marketing, then going to events and conventions with that focus should benefit me. However, if that isn't an area I want to focus on then going to those kinds of meetings will only create a spiritual or soul-pressure on me in directions that don't match where I am headed, which is unhelpful.

The Body of Christ is the same way. If I want miracles and power encounters, then I need to position myself and interact with others accordingly.

Before moving to Texas, I was on staff with a ministry in Portland, Oregon and we would host conferences and events that centered on the prophetic, healing, prayer, and the miraculous, all through the power of Jesus Christ. Naturally we would network with other ministries and at one point there was a big evangelistic crusade that one local ministry was hosting, and we were encouraged to attend. I did end up going to one meeting, but as a whole I avoided the event. Why? Not because evangelism is bad—it has its place. I was avoiding it because it isn't what God was doing with me in that season of my life and I didn't want the spiritual pull to do something that didn't fit the direction I was headed.

If we want to see miracles become regular in our lives, then we would be wise to get intentional about our time and energy. We would be far wiser to go to a conference or engage a ministry where miracles are happening and get impartation than we would to continue following our same weekly church routine and expecting something to suddenly change. If we want change, then we need to change things! We can receive from video recordings, audio messages, and books of miracle testimonies. We can receive and give away freely one to another and become living examples of the river in Ezekiel 47—where the more it flows the more it grows!

Impartation is really just a tool we can use to give and receive spiritual power, carrying it with us to new places, imparting it to new people, and cross-pollinating among the members of the Body of Christ. Imagine if instead of a regular gathering of just a handful of people doing this if there was a group of hundreds of sold-out believers pressing in together to apprehend the signs, wonders, and miracles God promised us. Consider what could happen if such a group regularly imparted one to another in order to help everyone break through into new levels in the spirit, expand their spiritual spheres of authority and power, and accelerate the pace at which they destroyed works of darkness in their area. So many have waited, fasted, and prayed for revival to come, but what if a seed of revival already lives within each of us? What if what we need to do is water those seeds, share them, and cultivate a culture of power where Christians actively and mightily destroy works of evil? What if this was a God-designed way that we could propel one another forward to see our prayers answered, miracles released, and our communities, cities, and nations transformed? I believe this is an under-utilized weapon in the kingdom of God to destroy the powers of darkness. In this hour God is releasing a new level of understanding to us so we can see and experience the Kingdom of Jesus Christ manifest more and more in the earth as it already is in heaven.

Works Cited

Braden, Gregg. *The Divine Matrix*. Carlsbad, CA: Hay House,
2007.

King, Michael C. *The Gamer's Guide to the Kingdom of God*.

Charleston: n.p., 2016. Print.

Strong, James. *Strong's Exhaustive Concordance*. Peabody, MA:
Hendrickson, 2007. Blueletterbible.com. Web. May. 2020.

Tan, Peter. *The Spiritual World*. Peter Tan Evangelism:

Canberra, AU 2007. PDF.

Stay Connected!

Thank you for reading The Power of Impartation. I hope this book has helped you gain a deeper level of understanding, revelation, and experience on this subject.

If you enjoyed this book, you can find more free content and other books I have written at www.thekingsofeden.com. You can also get a free gift for joining the mailing list to be notified of new products and events. Please consider leaving a review on Amazon.com so others can find this book more easily. God bless you!

Other titles by Michael King include:

Gemstones From Heaven - God Signs Series Book 1

Feathers From Heaven - God Signs Series Book 2

Faith to Raise the Dead - Abundant Life Series Book 1

The Gamer's Guide to the Kingdom of God

Practical Keys to Raise the Dead

Broken To Whole

God Speaks

About the Author

Michael King's love for God has given him a passion for signs, wonders, and miracles. By profession he is a Registered Nurse with a Masters in Nursing Education and it is his heart's desire to see the love of God transform and heal the pain in this world through power encounters with Jesus. Michael is married to a beautiful wife who doubles as his professional editor. You can find more of his writing on miracles, inner healing, faith, signs and wonders, and more on his website and blog, thekingsofeden.com and he is available for speaking engagements on request.

www.ingramcontent.com/pod-product-compliance
Lightning Source LLC
LaVergne TN
LVHW091303080426
835510LV00007B/377